PROVEN WORD books have proven themselves where it counts — among the thousands of readers who have made them best-sellers because they found them meaningful in the arena of life.

These books were best-sellers in hardcover and are now offered at a more affordable price in deluxe paperback bindings.

These special editions also offer you a built-in study guide with insightful questions which will encourage group discussions as well as personal reflection and thought.

The *Proven Word* series addresses the widespread needs of people everywhere who are searching for the answers to the pressures and problems of living in today's modern world.

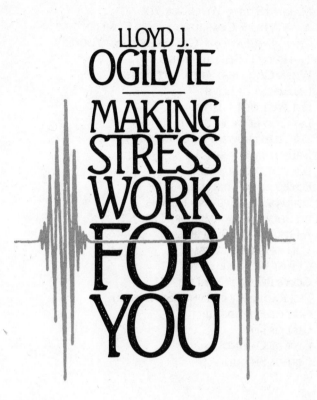

LLOYD J.
OGILVIE

MAKING
STRESS
WORK
FOR
YOU

Books by Lloyd J. Ogilvie

12 Steps to Living without Fear
The Other Jesus
If God Cares, Why Do I Still Have Problems?
Making Stress Work for You
Acts, Vol. 5, Communicator's Commentary
Congratulations, God Believes in You!
The Bush Is Still Burning
When God First Thought of You
Drumbeat of Love
Life without Limits
Let God Love You
The Autobiography of God
Jesus the Healer
Longing to Be Free
Loved and Forgiven
Lord of the Ups and Downs
If I Should Wake Before I Die
A Life Full of Surprises
You've Got Charisma
Cup of Wonder
God's Best for My Life
The Radiance of Inner Splendor
Gift of Friendship
Gift of Love
Gift of Caring
Gift of Sharing

LLOYD J. OGILVIE

MAKING STRESS WORK FOR YOU

Ten Proven Principles with Built-in Study Guide

WORD PUBLISHING
Dallas · London · Sydney · Singapore

Library of Congress Cataloging in Publication Data

Ogilvie, Lloyd John.
  Making stress work for you.

   1. Health—Religious aspects—Christianity.   2. Stress
(Psychology)   3. Emotions—Religious aspects—Christianity.
4. Bible.   N.T.   James—Criticism, interpretation, etc.
I. Title.
BT732.O35 1984   248.8′6   84–13219
ISBN 0–8499–3039–1

Printed in the United States of America

   98 RRD 9876

To

The Reverend Doctor James S. Stewart

a man in Christ
a prince of preachers
a communicator of grace

who, through the years since he was
my professor at New College, University
of Edinburgh, Scotland, has been a hero
in the faith, a constant inspiration, and
my friend

CONTENTS

PREFACE

SOME TIME AGO, I MADE A NATIONAL SURVEY OF what the American people perceived to be the greatest problems facing us today. I should not have been surprised that stress topped the list. That led me into a prolonged study of what stress actually is and how we can cope with it. As a person involved daily in trying to help people, I had observed not only their external sources of stress, but the internal stress they produced by their own thinking and reactions to life. I also got in touch with the external and internal causes of stress in my own life. My approach became one of a fellow struggler who needed answers as much or more than the people I wanted to help.

My search led me to try to define what is meant by the word *stress* and its many uses. Then I turned to the world of anatomy and medicine to develop an understanding of how the body reacts to stress. I devoured with avid interest the classical and contemporary writings of the most astute analysts of human nature. Turning next to the psychological disciplines to learn the linkage between thought and the control of emotional and physical reactions to external stress, I found that still something was missing. From my study I discovered the magnificent stress coping mechanism we have been given. Why was it not working for us?

My conclusion is that stress is essentially a spiritual problem. But it is more than believing, having faith, or saying our prayers. I had observed in myself and others who are committed Christians the same proclivity to inordinate stress reactions as in those who made no profession of faith in the Lord. In fact, I had to admit that guilt over having stress made many Christians more distressed than non-believers.

The more I studied the thinking portion of the brain, the special areas of cerebral cortex, and their interaction with the limbic system which controls our emotional response, I realized that areas of brain cortex had been created by the Lord to give us a grid which controls what gets into our nervous system. That led me to a prolonged study of how the Lord can actually indwell and control our thought processes, dominating our perception of what's happening around or to us.

We feel what we think. What we think about what happens around us is what triggers stress in us. When we are confronted by the dangers, difficulties or threats of life there is a split-second comprehension of them and then the signals are sent to our body to respond with fight or flight response. The same is true for the pressures of life. How we react is dependent on what our brain has signaled our bodies to do. Also, what we agree to assume is based on what we think. An overloaded life, filled with stress and potential burn-out, is the direct result of conscious choices guided by values and priorities which may not have been conditioned by our Lord.

Our reactions to people follow the same pattern. Until our thinking is conditioned with God's love and acceptance, we will physiologically react to the stress of competition, hostility, or impatience. The key to managing stress is allowing the Lord to indwell, condition, and control what happens in the cortex and the subcortical structures of our brain.

At the same time that I discovered this secret as the key to the control of stress, I was studying the Epistle of James. It suddenly hit me that James dealt with the major causes and cures of stress. Though he never uses the word, his advice about how to live life in Christ in a troubled world is really a very helpful stress management manual. The Epistle was written by James, Christ's brother, to Hebrew Christians around A.D. 50 in response to a very salient question: "If the Messiah has come, why is there no peace and tranquility?"

James's response is that the evidence of the Messianic Age is the Messiah's people.

The key of James is verse 1:18, "Of His own will He brought us forth by the word of truth, that we might be a kind of firstfruits of His creatures." Everything James has to say is for the purpose of encouraging the participants of the new creation that was made possible by Christ's life, death, resurrection, and indwelling power.

Jesus exemplified perfect unity of mind, body, and spirit, and He said that He had come to give us both abundant and eternal life. He promised that we would have abundant life here on earth if we were to abide in Him and He in us. And when He does abide in us, I believe the reasoning portion of our brain can be brought into unity with our physiologic systems which control the stress reactions to external stimuli.

I am amazed at the way James deals with the problems that modern medical science and psychiatry have helped us understand only recently. Though he did not possess a modern insight into neuroanatomy or our emotional responses, he addresses the causes and potential cures of stress that are so desperately needed today. By combining our knowledge of how we work physically and emotionally with what James has written, we discover ten crucial aspects of stress management.

He gives us the secret of managing stress by bringing thought, emotion and physical responses under the control of the mind of Christ, by showing us how to deal with anger creatively, how to express pent-up good intentions, how to communicate in a way that diffuses tension in us and others, how to overcome the envy that causes combative competition, how to re-order our priorities to accomplish our real purpose rather than be victimized by the demands of life and people, how to break free of the tyranny of things and money, how to discover and live on God's timing rather than in impatience and frustration, how to uti-lize meditation to draw on supernatural strength, and how to be encouraged by others who share with us the key to overcoming stress. And I believe that as we consider thoughtfully and prayerfully the message of James along with the insights of modern science, the Lord will give us a strategy for not only coping with stress but turning it into a source of strength.

It seems very clear to me now that the Lord created us to handle immense stress. But the stress manage-ment mechanism He gave us is dependent upon His indwelling presence and power. My hope is that we can discover how to use what He has endowed with His strength. If so, we will not only have found an answer to our own struggle with stress, but we will also have an answer for the most crucial, crippling problem confronting the twentieth century. Failure to learn how to cope with stress is a debilitating sickness of our time. The longed-for desire of managing it can be ours—to be experienced to the fullest, and then shared with others.

I am thankful for the many people who have helped me in the development of this book. Dr. Eliot Foltz, Associate Professor of Internal Medicine at Northwestern University Medical School and Past Governor of Northern Illinois for the American College of Physicians, has been a lifetime friend and consultant in my efforts to understand the linkage of the mind, body, and spirit in the healing of persons. Dr. H. J. Swan, eminent cardiologist, has been an encouraging friend and an immense help on the technical aspects of the anatomy of stress. Dr. Victor Herrmann, beloved physician and friend, has spurred me on with his medical knowledge and his commitment to the holistic approach to healing. Dr. Peter Dyck, Clinical Professor of Neurological Surgery at the University of Southern California, Dr. Richard Kasper, ophthalmological physician and surgeon, Dr. Charles Gahagen, physician in internal medicine, and Dr. Jean Gahagen, general practitioner, helped me in the use of technical medical language and were faithful in supporting this effort of their pastor in blending scientific and biblical truth.

Joyce Haman assisted me with helpful suggestions and editing and preparing the manuscript for submission to the publishers. Floyd Thatcher, Editor-in-Chief of Word, Inc., has been both mentor and friend in helping me through the years. His insights and guidance on this project have been invaluable. And to my Administrative Assistant, Jerlyn Gonzalez, goes deep gratitude for her enthusiasm for this book and her faithful typing of the manuscript for publication.

No book is finished when it leaves the author's hands. It then must have the careful editing of a competent person who has both grammatical and theological skills. I am pleased that Pat Wienandt, who has these skills and the gift of discernment, did the final editing.

To all of these cherished friends I express my appreciation and love.

LLOYD OGILVIE

CHAPTER ONE

THE SECRET OF
MANAGING STRESS

What makes some of us susceptible to the stress of certain kinds of people and situations? What are the unresolved conflicts that render us incapable of handling the pressures of life? Why do we do too much too long and finally burn out? What's driving us? What hostilities make us so impatient with ourselves and others? What insecurities make us inordinately competitive and angry? What is alarming is that when people discover the answers to these questions, or alter their lifestyle as a result, they still *suffer from stress.*

"STRESS, CAN WE COPE?"
This was the title of a lead article in *Time* magazine recently. It carried a thorough review of the epidemic proportions of stress in our society today.

Letters to the editor in subsequent issues were very revealing. One of them captured the reaction many of us have to much of the contemporary literature on stress. Rod Chandler, United States representative, wrote, "Before going to bed, I read your article on stress, then lay awake worrying about it. I see what you mean."

Articles and books on stress can be very *dis*tressing! They cause added stress about the danger of stress. Much is written in them about the causes of stress but not much about the cures. We are alarmed by elaborate graphs that show our diminishing life expectancy because of stress. We are told that many of the illnesses from which we suffer and will eventually die have been caused by our inability to cope with stress. Peptic ulcers, high blood pressure, certain strokes, migraines, asthma, neurodermatitis are all diagnosed as illnesses often produced by stress and our physiologic response to it.

Recent studies into its ability to depress the body's immune system, suggest that stress may also lower our resistance to communicable diseases such as colds and flu, and, more serious, may influence the development of cancer.

Detailed questionnaires published to help us tabulate our vulnerability to stress disturb us further. The analysis of the causes of stress is a disarming look in the mirror as we are forced to see what the pressures of life on the fast track are doing to us.

The results of these questionnaires expose our vulnerability to stress with incisive honesty. And we see the brashness of our combatively competitive life in the asphalt jungle depicted with frightening clarity. Yet, few subjects have produced more rhetoric and less remedial help than stress. The diagnosis is telling, the prognosis is terrifying, and the prescriptions are tenuous.

When solutions are offered they are often simplistic, only patching but never healing the wound. We are told to relax. Slow down before we break down. Do less and live longer. Stay out of stress-producing situations. Avoid stressful people. Take more vacations. Get some fun in your life. Sit in a hot tub. Use a bio-feedback machine to lower your muscle tension. Express your anger, cry more, join a therapy group. Get more exercise, balance your diet, drink less caffeine. The list of temporary remedies grows longer every day as we struggle to find some answer for stress—the personal and public enemy Number One of our time.

The medical profession has rallied its resources and research to confront the growing problem. Medical centers and schools have separate departments dedicated to stress research. We now have elaborate and explicit explanations of how the nervous system works to combat external stress. Pharmaceuticals have been developed to deal with its destructive effects. The best-selling drugs on the market today are the tranquilizer Valium, the cardiac drug Inderal, and the ulcer medication Tagamet. But these are utilized after stress has already taken its toll on the body. Now medical research scientists are concentrating their efforts on a search for some drug that might actually block the body's physiologic response to external stress.

Meanwhile psychiatrists have joined the battle against stress by investigating the psychodynamic reasons why we respond to it the way we do. What makes some of us susceptible to the stress of certain kinds of people and situations? What are the unresolved conflicts that render us incapable of handling the pressures of life? Why do we do too much too long and finally burn out? What's driving us? What hostilities make us so impatient with ourselves and others? What insecurities make us inordinately competitive and angry? What is alarming is that when people discover the answers to these questions, or alter their lifestyle as a result, they *still* suffer from stress.

Industry is equally alarmed by the effects of stress on its employees. Physical and emotional problems resulting from it have caused a mounting problem of executive burnout and absenteeism at all levels. This has prompted large grants from corporations to study how to overcome stress. Some companies have hired consultants to work with the problem. And others have developed programs for physical exercise, more consistent vacation breaks, and psychiatric counseling for employees.

Stress has become an expensive liability to efficient production. The costs have been estimated to be as high as seventy-five billion dollars a year, about seven hundred and fifty dollars for every worker. The major contributing factor is stress-related sickness.

What can we do about stress? A couple of years ago that question became intensely personal for me. Three things converged on me at the same time and made me determined to find an answer. My wife was at that time recovering from cancer. One day she startled me by saying, "Lloyd, I am convinced that my cancer was induced by stress." She went on to share with me the conclusion about the contributing factors to her sickness that she, her counselor who was helping her through post-operative adjustments, and her oncologist had made.

I must have looked shocked and defensive, and I was. How could *my* wife be under stress? As we talked, I became aware of what a negative word *stress* was in my mind. It was synonymous with lack of trust and strength. I had preached about stress and how belief in God made us exempt from its impact. Now I had to take another look. After all, my wife believed in God, prayed, and lived a healthy life. And yet, the stresses of life—raising a family, being a community leader, and participating in our taxing, busy life—had affected her health. That forced me to look deeper into the causes and cures of stress, not just for people I'm trying to help, but for me and my family.

The second contributing factor to my intense concern about stress came to light one day when my personal physician read me the report of my complete physical examination. "Magnificent!" he mused as he looked over the charts and the results of the test.

I relaxed and said, "Thanks a lot!"

"You've misunderstood me," he went on. "You are magnificently made; my hope is that the stress you're living with won't get you down." Then he went on to explain that the reports were all good, but knowing me, he was concerned about my schedule, my tendency to be overconscientious, and the pressure of counseling people. Being a sensitive diagnostician, he had discovered the first telltale signs of stress wearing on me.

I was shocked. My image of myself as a Christian was that I was impervious to the stress under which I saw others suffering. At that point I determined to discover all I could about stress, particularly how it could affect a person who had faith in God. The experience made me all the more empathetic to what my wife was discovering. Also, I became much more sensitive to what stress was doing to my congregation and friends. That same year, two of my close friends had died of coronary heart disease, both illnesses induced by stress. Believe me, the subject of stress had my attention!

The third factor was less personal, but no less powerful. Just about the time all of this was going on I was beginning a television ministry. In an attempt to make it a program that addressed pertinent problems instead of being a one-way conversation, as so many religious programs are, I asked the viewers to write me what they perceived to be the greatest problem facing the American people so that I could build my messages as a personal answer.

The responses came tumbling in by the mailbagful. As I read them, I discovered that stress topped the list. People, most of whom were Christians, confessed that stress was their greatest problem. Now I knew I had to address the problem of stress. But because of my personal encounters with it, I knew I would have to do so as a fellow struggler, not as one who gave simplistic, guilt-producing, "ought" admonitions. In preparation, I made a prolonged investigation of stress that led me into an in-depth study of the neurophysiology and psychodynamics of stress. It was during that investigation that I discovered the main thrust of what I want to say in this book. It has changed my life. I hope for nothing less for you.

My study began with a search for a definition of the word *stress*. The word has become a catchall synonym for the pace, pressure, and problems of life. We talk about being under stress, facing stressful situations, and dealing with stress-producing people. We have a general understanding of what causes stress, but too little knowledge of how to live with it. I discovered that the word for stress in Latin is *strictus*, "to be drawn tight." In Old French it is *estresse*, meaning narrowness or tightness. In English a clear definition of stress is complicated by its many different uses. However, in the worlds of physics and mechanics it is used both for the forces which cause external pressure and for the internal strength to balance them.

In the parlance of physics, for example, stress is a technical term for the measurement of weight strain on materials. On the other hand, in mechanics the word *stress* is used for the internal strength of a metal to withstand an imposed weight load. And it is interesting to note that stress capacity on metals is measured by what is called yield point or failure point.

Yield point is the point at which the stress on the material actually makes it stronger; the failure point is the point at which the strain exceeds the load-bearing capacity of the material. I believe the same is true of human beings. External stress can strengthen our internal coping system, but extreme stress will bring us to failure or breaking point.

Medical science also has its special definition of stress. In response to external stress, the nervous system provides the needed energy to meet the responsibilities, pressures, crises, and alarms of life.

It is fascinating to consider how it works. Three parts of our nervous system participate in "stress management": the cerebral cortex, the limbic system, and the autonomic nervous system. Now, I know these are technical medical terms, but bear with me, because an understanding of how these function helps us to see that we have been provided with a marvelous capacity to respond to external stimuli.

The brain cortex is the center of many of our conscious mental or intellectual functions such as thinking, memory, imagination, fantasizing, dreaming, talking, and association. It also controls motor activity, physical coordination and the sensory functions of sight, hearing, touch, taste, and smell. On the other hand, the limbic system controls in part the emotional responses of our bodies as well as the physiologic reflex functions, appetites, drives, heartbeat, and breathing. Crucial parts of the limbic system are the hypothalamus, the pituitary, the adrenal, and other endocrine glands which are responsible for the level of substances in the blood called hormones. The cortex interacts with the limbic system, which in turn activates the endocrine and other body systems to provide the hormonal level required to meet the external demands of life. The late Dr. Hans Selye, an eminent authority on stress, has called this process the "general adaptation system."

When we are hit with either the dangers or difficulties of life, our cortex goes into "red alert." Then the limbic system responds with a "ready for action" flow of chemicals known as neurotransmitters, which include the catecholamines. Among other delayed side effects there may be an increased level of cholesterol in the blood. The "agitated" period may last as long as seventy-two hours.

Unfortunately, many of us live in a constant state of "red alert" because of the pressures or problems we face. One seventy-two hour alert is piled on top of another. And added to the external causes that prompt a "red alert" are the memory and imagination resident within the brain. This means that we keep our bodies in a state of emergency long after the crisis has passed.

The physical reaction triggered by these successions of stress alerts put us into a dangerous continuing state of high arousal, a physiologic overdrive. The blood hormone levels remain abnormal, blood pressure stays high; fat metabolism (cholesterol production) and clotting elements that have been triggered to meet the high state of stress persist. Consequently, we become susceptible to a variety of health problems including high blood pressure, stroke, and heart attacks. Recent medical studies have shown excessive lipids (fatty components) in the blood of people living under persistent great stress.

In other words, the thoughts formed in the cortex, the "conscious brain," determine the responses of the limbic system, the "instinctive brain." Our gift of intellect can be a liability unless we develop a basis of understanding life and its pressures. The cerebral cortex must become a computer that sorts out the stresses of life and controls the degree of arousal of the limbic system—"For as he thinks in his heart, so is he" (Prov. 23:7, NKJV). It is imperative that we discover a way to regulate our reaction to the threats and trials of life so that we do not keep our bodies in a constant state of readiness for "fight or flight." How we accomplish it is what I want to share with you, based on my own personal experience.

Here is the good news—you can manage stress! The Lord has endowed you and me with a stress management mechanism that gives us an immense capacity for coping with the pressures and problems of life. We do not have to be the helpless victims of stress-producing situations, people, or circumstances. We have been given an inner ability to handle the external pressures of life.

The secret to the effective use of our God-given stress-management system—cerebral function, limbic system, interaction, and autonomic adaptation—is somehow mysteriously linked to our relationship to God. He created us for Himself—to experience His love and power, and to love, glorify, and serve Him in response. But, He wanted our relationship with Him to be more than His manipulation of a race of marionettes. Therefore he gave us freedom of choice—the free will to respond or resist the fellowship He created us to have with Him. When we choose to walk closely with the Lord, His reorienting, transforming power influences the thoughts of the cortex. When we *will* to run our own lives and make our choices without His guidance, however, our thinking brain is left to its own choices to respond to the stress-producing stimuli of life. Without His Spirit to infuse the tissues of our brains with wisdom, knowledge, and truth, our own strength and coping ability are limited.

The cerebral cortex, as the grid controlling what gets into the rest of our nervous system and eventually into our blood, is then dependent upon only *our* perceptions of what is good or bad for us. We make decisions that may lead to troublesome situations, and we evaluate life's dangers and threats on the basis of our own ability to face and conquer hostile forces. We try to manage life on our own, be good by our own efforts, and stabilize our relationships with our own adequacy and power to control people and life around us.

Just the opposite usually happens. The pressures of life and the values and opinions of people control our thinking. Our culture too often determines what we think is important and how we react. We become overly dependent on people's approval and often shape our lives to please them. As a result, we end up in a "stress mess."

The alternative to this is a personal, intimate relationship with the Lord in which He guides our thoughts and reactions. He designed us to be able to receive and implement His will for us. To accomplish that, He implants in our brains the thoughts which are His best for us.

Deep fellowship with Him results in a transformation of our perception of who we are, what we are to be, and what is most creative for us to do. Our thinking becomes focused in the truth that we are loved and forgiven. We realize our purpose is to be communicators of His love to others, and that frees us from being combative or overly conciliatory. People are not threats to be subdued, but persons to be loved and encouraged. And the problems people cause then become challenges to be met with the guidance and perseverance the Lord will provide. Without a pervading conviction that we are loved by the Lord, the words and actions, slights and oversights, rejection and hostility, distress and angers of others will trigger a physiological chain reaction that will send surges of destructive stress charging through our bodies.

The liberating news is that the God who created us took the responsibility to recreate us. Christ came from the heart of God not only to reveal His unchanging love but to provide a basis of a reorienting transformation of our thinking brain. The Gospel of John tells us that Christ is the Word of God through whom all things were created in the beginning. The One through whom we were made came to remake us. He revealed who God is, but also what we were meant to be.

Here in history, walking among us, was the perfect incarnation of God's original purpose. His life revealed what we were created to be spiritually, intellectually, emotionally, and physically. His message was filled with truth about God and how to put Him and His kingdom, His rule and reign, first in our thinking, acting, and reacting. Everywhere Jesus went, He proclaimed healing truth about God's love, forgiveness, and power as the basis of our wholeness as people. He called us back to the essentials given to Israel long before—to love the Lord God with all our heart, soul, and might (Deut. 6:5)—and added the crucial dimension of loving Him with our minds (Matt. 22:37).

During the few years of His ministry, Jesus saw the debilitating result of distorted and twisted thinking. In addition, He saw that the bondage of sin so enslaved the human will, producing such a resistance to God that a life of true freedom in fellowship with Him was greatly diminished. Then, to save us from the stress of this confused perception of who we are and Whose we are, He went to the cross to atone for our sins of rebellion. The heart of God, Immanuel, God with us, suffered the anguish of Calvary to provide a basis for our forgiveness and for the reconciliation and healing of our estranged minds.

Two days after His crucifixion Jesus was raised from the dead. For forty days the risen Lord remained with His followers continuing His ministry and teaching His central theme of the kingdom of God. We are astounded that being with Christ and witnessing the power of His resurrection did not accomplish the purpose for which He had come. The disciples rejoiced over His victory over death, but did not realize the full impact of what He had done for them. They had seen life in its fullness in the Master, but could not live it.

Some of the most stressful days recorded in the New Testament are captured in the first chapter of Acts. Christ was alive, but the disciples were impotent to follow His leading and commission. Many of us can identify with their condition. When Christ ascended, He left behind a band of followers filled with the stress of trying to be faithful on their own strength. It's a terrible frustration to have a vision without the power to live it.

Then, on the great day of Pentecost, Christ returned in the power of the Holy Spirit to fill the disciples with Himself. The One who had lived among them now lived His life in and through them. The transformation of their minds for which He lived, died, and rose became profoundly personal. From within them, He generated new people, reorienting their minds, remolding their characters, and rejuvenating their courage and strength. A new creation began with new creatures in whom Christ would dwell. The stress of confused thinking, human inadequacy, and equivocating unwillingness was replaced by the Lord's indwelling wisdom, love, and guidance.

What does all that have to do with our battle with stress today? Everything! Jesus Christ wants to take up residence in us. The port of entry is our spirit. His love, revealed on the cross, enables us to open ourselves to His indwelling. Then He heals our rebellious, imperious wills to enable us to do His will for our lives. The tissues of our cerebral cortex can now be reoriented so we can think His thoughts. Now the Lord becomes the grid of our thinking brain, monitoring what passes through to our nervous system. What we see, hear, and perceive through the complex system connected to our brain can be brought under His control.

I know what that means. The experience of stress in my own life has been radically transformed. At one point in my growth as a Christian I discovered the power of not only abiding in Christ to receive His love and forgiveness, but also of inviting Him to abide in me to reform my thinking about myself, about my life, goals, and the pressures of daily experience, and about death. Up to that time I muddled in the stress mess. I was a victim of countless fears, insecurities, and anxieties. There was no control over what got into my nervous system. I was helpless to control the stress that pulsed in my body, leaving me agitated and then exhausted.

As I mentioned in the Preface, at this same time I was studying the Epistle of James and I suddenly realized that James deals with the major causes and cures of stress and his epistle is really a very helpful stress management manual.

Let me repeat just a few words of background. James's Epistle was written to Hebrew Christians around A.D. 50 in response to the question: "If the Messiah has come, why is there no peace and tranquility?" James's response is that the evidence of the messianic age is to be found in the Messiah's people—the new people of God: "Of His own will He brought us forth by the word of truth that we might be a kind of firstfruits of His creatures" (James 1:18). James's remarkable little letter has for its prime purpose the encouragement of the participants of the new creation that is made possible by Christ's life, death, resurrection, and indwelling power.

A Christian is one who has received Christ's message about the abundant life and His power to live it. We are to be examples of life as it was meant to be lived in a stress-filled world. James sounds the same call to new life in an old world that was later expressed by Paul to the Corinthians. "Therefore, if anyone is in Christ, he is a new creation; old things have passed away; behold, all things have become new" (2 Cor. 5:17).

Christ came to set us free of the stress syndrome. He assumed our human nature and went to the cross to reconcile us with God *and* to heal our troubled minds. The cosmic atonement of Calvary made possible a new creature, a new breed of humanity, people in whom Jesus Christ could live His victorious post-resurrection, Pentecost life. And we can be certain that when we abide in Christ as Savior and Lord and He abides in us as unifying, reorienting power, we can live the abundant life now and eternal life forever. We can receive the mind of Christ in our brain and thought process. Further, we know that when He dominates our thinking, our perspective on reality is changed radically, with the result that our God-given stress-management capability, particularly the function of the limbic system, is controlled by His patience and peace.

But the question remains, why do so many Christians still have an inordinate amount of stress reactions? The answer, I believe, is found in the truth that it is possible to believe in Christ as our Savior and yet never allow Him to be the indwelling anointer of our minds. James tells us many ways to receive that anointing as an antidote to stress.

Right in the first chapter of this little book, we read a rather mind-boggling statement about how to react to "trials"—and that could well be translated "stresses." "Count it all joy when you fall into various trials, knowing that the testing of your faith produces patience. But let patience have its perfect work, that you may be perfect and complete, lacking nothing. If any of you lacks wisdom, let him ask of God, who gives to all liberally and without reproach, and it will be given to him. But let him ask in faith, with no doubting, for he who doubts is like a wave of the sea driven and tossed by the wind. For let not that man suppose that he will receive anything from the Lord; he is a double-minded man, unstable in all his ways" (James 1:2–8). From this amazing word we discover that the first secret of stress management is to think about stress as a source of joy! That requires a new perspective, a different way of thinking. When Christ indwells our thinking, transforming our way of looking at life, we can then see the sources of stress as a prelude to a deeper experience of joy.

In the midst of stress we are challenged to "count it all joy." The Greek word for "count" comes from the verb meaning to consider, to think. And the implication of these words is that once and for all, now and forever, we are challenged to think through our trials—our stresses—until we perceive them as a source of deeper joy.

What an amazing insight! But look at it this way. The causes of stress are in what might be called the five "C's": change, conflict, criticism, concerns, and crises. Add to these an overbooked schedule, unresolved tensions, and a troubled conscience, and we have a stress-filled life. But we also have the possibility of greater dependence on the Lord for guidance and the assurance of His intervention in our needs.

Joy is the result of grace. The two words come from the same root in Greek. When Christ's mind controls the cerebral cortex we know that we are loved regardless of what happens to us or around us. The stresses of life are the negatives that release the positives. They can be either the occasion of deeper trust, with the release of fresh grace, or the source of frustration. When we surrender our stresses to Christ, He uses them for our growth and His glory. We know that He will neither leave us nor forsake us. Joy springs forth from that artesian reservoir of grace. We *can* turn stress into a stepping stone! It all depends on how we think about it.

A converted cortex becomes the grid that guards the nervous system. Under the control of the mind of

Christ, what is signaled to the limbic system is radically altered. What would cause others to go into "red alert" is changed into a challenge to be faced with Christ's help.

Patience is a good word to describe how this works. Patience is Christ's perspective on perplexities. In Him we perceive the shortness of this life and the length of eternity. And each stress is confronted in the light of its potential for greater trust and the experience of greater strength.

"The testing of our faith produces patience." James's word for "testing" in Greek means proof. The genuine authenticity of our faith in Christ is revealed by how we confront and deal with life's stresses and strains. If life were free totally of any stress, we would never need the infusion of Christ's strength. The point is that when stress does hit us we can know that Christ is adequate for all needs.

James forces us to see our trials in the perspective of our ultimate purpose: "But let patience have its perfect work, that you may be perfect and complete, lacking in nothing." The word "perfect" in Greek comes from a word meaning "end" or "goal." We are to see, think through, each stress situation in the light of our own purpose and destination. We are alive forever, heaven is our destination, and on the way we can deal with the frustrations of life knowing that they ultimately do not matter. And each of them can be turned into growth in becoming the person we were meant to be.

The special gift of a Christ-controlled cortex is wisdom, the mind of the Lord. "If any of you lacks wisdom, let him ask of God, who gives liberally and without reproach, and it will be given him." The word for "lack" is an ancient banking term for insufficient funds—or an overdrawn account. When stress strains our resources, we can ask for wisdom, and the Lord will respond with exactly what we need. The word James uses for "liberally" in Greek also means single-minded. For me that implies that the Lord specifically gives us perspective on each of our stresses and He gives us His strength to endure them. He matches our output with His input. We can have balanced accounts. He puts in what we must put out!

The opposite of this is doubt and a double mind. The deeper meaning of the words could describe a malfunctioning nervous system. To doubt, in James's context, means to separate. The Greek word is *diakrinō—dia* meaning "between"; *krinō*, "separate." Doubt here implies the separation of the trial or stress from the Lord's providence, power, and purpose. It is to question His ability to use stress—the complete antithesis of faith which trusts our affairs to Him. That kind of fragmented thinking floods our body with distress, with a constant "red alert" as we try to handle life on our own.

The word James coined for a fragmented mind is "double-minded." It is *dispsuchos—dis*, "twice"; *psuchē*, "soul." A double mind is divided, where thought and response are wrenched apart, or where thought does not control the reactions of our total nervous system and its functions. We are divided from Christ's plan and perspective, and we seek to run our own lives. Now we are in for an even greater stress than the world can produce. It is the stress of resisting the Lord's Spirit. There is no greater distress than imperious self-will. It sets up a jangling static in our total being. Nothing works right. We become engulfed in the stress mess.

So the first step in managing stress is to invite Christ to dwell in our minds, becoming the director of the master control center. The result will be a conviction of His grace and a joyous attitude in our stress. Our stress will become what Dr. Hans Selye calls "eustress"—good stress. The prefix *eu* in Greek means good or well. The Lord can turn stress into a source of His strength.

CHAPTER TWO

HOW TO BE GOOD
AND ANGRY

My own experience convinces me that intense feelings of frustration, and the consequent triggering of the emotion of anger and the agitation of our nervous system, can be altered. When that happens, the expression of our anger or indignation can be turned to more important issues than resentment over the denial of our needs.

TELL ME WHAT TICKS YOU OFF, AND I WILL TELL you what makes you tick. Tell me what has made you angry and I will tell you the needs in your life you perceive are being frustrated. Anger is the strong emotional reaction to the frustration of our needs.

By needs I mean what we think is necessary for our happiness. These are a combination of what we consider right, good, and creative for us. These basics are expressed in our desires, drives, goals, and plans for ourselves and for the people we love. Topping these are our beliefs, values, and convictions about what should happen to and around us.

Our needs form what I like to call the "indignation index" in our cerebral cortex, the thinking part of our brain. Each factor in the computer of our brain has been established there by experience, conditioning, and training. Each forms the fabric of who we are and what we want from life. The stronger the strands of this fabric, the greater our self-identity and determination become in shaping the relationships and direction of our lives. We know what we want, when we want it, how we want it, and with whom we want it.

When any one of our needs is blocked, challenged, contradicted, or delayed, a charge is set off in our indignation index and we perceive denial. That sends a message to the limbic system, which in turn reacts with the emotion of anger and floods our bloodstream with agitation. It makes our "blood boil," as we say. The limbic system prepares for battle. "Red alert" is signaled, and the blood surges with hormones to equal the challenge of a Custer's last stand.

Dr. Abraham Maslow tells us that there is a graduated spectrum of our needs. In *The Psychology of Being*, he describes the basic needs of life—safety and security, belongingness and affection, respect and self-respect, and self-actualization. When any of these is stifled, we become angry. We feel that inside ourselves. We can also observe it in the anger of people around us and in our society as a whole. Everything from tantrums, seething pouts, and outbursts to riots results. Friendships can be broken by this anger, marriages strained, production in our jobs debilitated, and effective progress in society ground to a halt.

We live in an angry world. We feel it in the discontent crystalized in the major issues that swirl around us and in the violence of groups and individuals who are frustrated because their needs have not been met. When we are relatively satisfied for a brief time, we still feel the impact of the anger of others and then internalize the stress it produces.

The other day I heard a radio announcement advertising a television program called *The Sons of Corfu*. With passion in his voice, the announcer said, "If you want to get your anger out, if you want to feel vindictive, watch this program." Amazing! But so many of the popular television programs trigger our indignation index. They display anger and violence and broken relationships, and the negation of human need incites our anger. I believe that in watching them many people get a vicarious release of their pent-up anger at the frustration of their own needs. Television executives who plan and produce what we are offered day and night tell me that the display of anger in human relationships sells. As one programmer of a major network told me, "People are angry inside, but they don't know how to express it, and they get some relief from watching television dramas and soaps where people do."

Certainly, we are all eager to find a means of expressing our indignation over the frustration of our needs in a way that does not cause debilitating stress in us or the people or groups who have caused it.

But empathizing with someone else's anger really doesn't help us with our own. And suppressing our anger doesn't help either.

I talked to a woman recently who was very depressed. Knowing from long personal experience and extensive study of depression, I wondered what was making her angry. What needs were being frustrated? I knew she was a deeply committed Christian but I also knew that she prided herself in always being in control of herself. She displayed a mask of Christian love and happiness. Her composure was always outwardly impeccable.

"What's been making you angry lately?" I asked. Her response conveyed surprise and indignation. "Angry?" she said forcefully. "I never get angry!" She was angry at me for even suggesting she might not be in complete control of herself and everything in her life.

So I put it another way. "Anything been upsetting you recently?"

That was a bit less threatening to her. "Yes, but I want you to know I never get angry!" Her body language contradicted what she said as she crossed her legs, tightly folded her arms across her chest, furrowed her brow, and tightened her lips. What I had asked touched a raw nerve and I could see the outward signs of stress surging in her body.

I waited in silence. Suddenly she pounded her fist on the coffee table in front of the couch where she was sitting, jumped up, stamped her foot, and began pacing. Mrs. Composed was feeling and expressing anger. Now, for some reason, she seemed to feel safe and could allow her suppressed emotions to fly without fear, and she went on to tell me about her husband's neglect and the inconsiderate attitudes of her children. "All I do is give, give, give and all they do is take, take, take! I've got needs, too, you know!"

My response was to agree with the obvious. We all have needs. They are not wrong. They are ours, and we feel them acutely. But we cannot submerge them forever or suppress them behind some false image of composure. This woman had trapped herself: the need to project the image of control had superseded the need to express her own feelings of loneliness, lack of affection and of being appreciated. There was nothing to do but turn the anger in on herself, and her feelings of depression had resulted.

I tell this story not to add another soap drama to those already bombarding us on television, but to expose the vital link between the denial of our needs to the stress it causes—and the resultant depression.

After getting her to talk out her needs and how they were being denied, I could then lead the woman through a creative discussion of how to express her needs more creatively. The more we talked, the more she realized that her anger was not wrong. The person who was wrong was her mother who had ingrained into her thinking that "nice girls never get angry!" She confided that she remembered her mother's voice always sounded angry when pounding that idea into her repeatedly through her growing years. She had taken on a "Christian countenance" that did not match her uncertain spirituality within.

The woman's husband had married her because he said she was always so pleasant, never lost her temper, and was constantly agreeable. And he had reminded her of this through the years, especially when he wanted to be sure she reacted passively to his busy schedule, his attentiveness to other women, and his need to have his home a retreat from the pressures of life. The few times she had expressed her needs, his reaction was so angry that it frightened her and she withdrew.

As we talked, I was able to help this woman see the challenge of finding a way of expressing her needs and allowing her husband and children to grow up. She came to see the need to love herself enough to do that creatively, and that required a deeper sense of God's love for her. She admitted that her greatest need was for His love and acceptance, that her inner feeling of being valued, cherished, and held in esteem had to come from Him. No human relationship could fill the God-shaped emptiness in her soul. She now realized she had spent so much time and effort pretending to be a "good Christian" that she had neglected her primary relationship with God.

We then prayed together, and after accepting God's love, she asked Him to show her ways she could relate to her loved ones and how she could express her needs in a way they could understand. In a later conversation she confided that the direction she received in her subsequent prayers was simply to tell her husband and children how she was feeling, to share her false idea of peace at any price, and to let them know how those attitudes affected her. She saw that the key was not to blame them, but to admit that she was the cause of the problem. Slowly she came to understand that it would be okay to cry and open her heart. But even more important, she was guided to tell them how lonely she felt and how much she needed their love and encouragement.

It worked. Because she did not make accusations, her husband listened without an outburst, and her honest sharing of herself melted his resistance. The confession of loneliness behind her adequacy mask shocked him into a realization of his attitudes and feelings. He was able then to tell her that he never felt needed, that his deepest need was for a wife who didn't seem to have it "all put together" and who really wanted his attention and affection. He then confessed that her serene, perfectionist attitude made her come through as a cold person, and that made him feel unnecessary and put off. The thought of a wife who needed him, desired him, and wanted profound intimacy in sharing deepest feelings and thoughts as well as unrestrained sexual passion, put him in touch with unmet needs in his life. And he told her about the times he wished he had been married to someone else and how much this upset him. Fortunately, his attentiveness to women who thought he was great never had gone too far, but he could now admit to his wife how tempted he had been.

This initial confrontation and mutual expression of needs was followed by many deep conversations in the days that followed. The sharing of deep, inner feelings created an atmosphere of romance and began a honeymoon much more exciting than the strained one they had had twenty years before. Now, two people who had missed each other for all those years found delight and satisfaction in each other.

On the other hand, the attitudes that had developed with and by the teenage children had to be handled differently. "Poor mom-ism" would not be creative or remedial. A whole new style of life was called for, and in this, the woman's husband led the way. Formerly, his own unexpressed anger toward her had been communicated in negative attitudes that the children had picked up and followed.

Now the father assumed the role of leadership he had previously abdicated, and he talked with the children about their mother and set the example for their acceptance of her and their expressions of affirmation. At the same time, the mother's change of attitude and her openness in expressing her needs and in telling the children how much she needed them began to have a positive effect on the mood in the home. And she became free to express her anger in creative ways that helped the children see she really cared about them. That freed them to express anger about frustrations they were feeling with friends, at school, and in their own battle for self-esteem. Now, instead of reproducing over and over again the problem her mother had foisted on her, this woman broke the chain of repeating the past by treating her own children as she had been treated by her mother. As the children began to learn how to be honest with their feelings, they discovered from their changed parents that anger can be expressed creatively, without attack or blame.

I believe this story is an excellent example of how we can act to balance the scale which is so often weighted on the side of the misuse of anger with its resultant stress. The story of this family does leave us with some perplexing questions, however. What needs of ours are being frustrated in the family, at work, or in our busy round of activities? Are we trying to satisfy our ultimate need for God in people, projects, or possessions? And after we have allowed Him to love us profoundly with acceptance and esteem as His chosen and called persons, have we asked Him to guide us in communicating our needs in a way that does not produce blame and guilt in others?

My own experience convinces me that intense feelings of frustration, and the consequent triggering of the emotion of anger and the agitation of our nervous system, can be altered. When that happens, the expression of our anger or indignation can be turned to more important issues than resentment over the denial of our needs.

In the Gospel story we read that Jesus got angry. But He never got angry over people's reaction to Him. His anger always came in response to the neglect of human needs or the blasphemous use of religion to resist God. He was angry at the Pharisees who questioned His Sabbath-day healing of the man with the withered hand. He was angered by the abuse of the temple and drove the money changers out. But, on the other hand, He was infinitely patient with His disciples who were slow to follow and reticent to learn, who vied with each other for power, denied Him, and betrayed Him. There was no anger on the cross, and after the Resurrection, there was only persistence to help His followers overcome their fear.

The Lord's brother, James, learned much from Him about how to deal with anger. What he has to say in his epistle to the early church gives us an antidote to uncreative anger and the stress it causes us. In that epistle we see that the Lord can help us sort out the difference between righteous indignation and our petulant hostility rooted in self-centeredness. We learn that the cycle can be broken between the perception of the frustration of a need and the uncontrolled expression of the emotion, as well as the turbulent stirring of our hormonal balance. And we discover the need to be more concerned about our right relationship with the Lord than about always being "right" in our human relationships and constantly having to defend our rights against possible misuse by others.

James is very practical again in his stress manual. "Therefore, my beloved brethren, let every man be swift to hear, slow to speak, slow to wrath; for the wrath of man does not produce the righteousness of God" (James 1:19–20). In these words we are given three checks for the management of stress-producing anger.

The first is to be "swift to hear." Listening is one of the crucial aspects of the thinking capacity of the cortex. We listen with both ears and eyes. The optic nerve and the auditory nerve send our impressions of reality to the cortex. There it is sorted out and given meaning on the basis of previous conditioning, learning, and experience. When what we see or hear triggers a negative impact on our desires, plans, and values, as well as beliefs and convictions, the cortex sends its interpretation to the limbic system. It also modifies what we say or do in expression of that anger. If, for example, the thinking of our cortex tells the limbic system that we dislike what we have seen and heard and believe we have been dealt with unfairly, the limbic system then responds with the emotion of anger, accompanied by a sympathetic release of body chemicals. Our changed physical state affects the capacity of the cortex to control our thinking, speaking, and other conscious intellectual, sensory, and motor functions.

When we are told by James to be "quick to listen" he means that we are to be sure we hear and observe both what's said and what's implied—we are able to "read between the lines." A Christ-controlled person listens and sees with His ears and eyes. When our basic needs are being satisfied by Christ, we get less angry and are better able to handle the slights and oversights of others. We become more concerned about soul-sized issues, and our indignation is ignited by righteous causes rather than self-centered concerns.

Then, too, prayer is a part of listening—to people and to the Lord. When we share with Him the things we've heard or seen which make us angry, we can then respond with His love and creative concern. Our task is to talk to Him about our angers before we tell others about them. Jim Rayburn, the founder of Young Life, often reminded his workers with high school students that they had to earn the right to be heard. The same would be true in expressing our angers creatively. People will not hear us unless they know that we love them. Any authentic anger we may feel must be expressed in the context of a relationship of assurance and affirmation. Then we can say, "This is how I'm feeling. Please hear me because what I am saying is a part of my love for you."

Next, being "slow to speak" follows naturally. We don't have to blurt out our angers immediately. Words can cut and hurt irreparably. A part of prayer over our anger is to get the Lord's perspective, then

His timing, and then His attitude. Above all, our expression of anger need not multiply an endless cycle of mounting hostility.

Recently I heard a man say, "I really feel like getting good and angry." What he meant was that he felt like being really angry. I said, "If you are to be good and angry at the same time, you'll need the Lord's help."

We all do. Have you ever awakened in the early hours of the morning and thought back on your all-too-quick, angry retort to someone? I have! Those times make me all the more committed to waiting until I have the Lord's perspective, patience, and power for my reply. And those experiences have led to a commitment that has lowered my stress level. It is the commitment to ask people who say or do disturbing, anger-producing things to repeat what they've said, or to request that they explain to me why they did what they did. This gives me time not only to listen carefully, but to pray inside, "Lord, help me to respond with Your mind controlling mine and Your attitude guiding both the tone and intent of my words." These few moments keep me from blurting out a crippling response.

At a conference recently I failed at that, but I learned from it. During the course of the meeting I had tried to be very open and vulnerable in communicating my feelings and my message. I laid myself open and talked about how I was experiencing healing in my own life. Most of my listeners affirmed that, and we experienced the closeness of fellow strugglers in whom the Lord was attempting a fresh surge of power—all except one woman.

She came up to me one afternoon and said, "I think this is *going to be* a great conference. My only hope is that you will pull out all the stops and let us know you!"

Without pausing, I responded, "Pull out all the stops? What do you think I've been doing?" Then I commented directly to her about her critical attitude, but I realized later that I did it in the wrong way. So all she got was the impact of my impatience and anger. Since she had a fragile ego and low self-esteem, what I said really hurt her.

When I reflected on my response later, I realized that she was trying to express a desire in her own life to pull out the stops and be open. If I had given the Lord a chance to intervene and had asked for His help in responding, I probably would have said, "We all want to pull out the stops. Thanks for expressing your hope for me. I've tried to do that so far and will do even more with your prayers and support. Somehow I have the feeling that what you want for me also expresses a deep need in your own life. Tell me about how you're doing in responding to the Lord's power. I really want to know so I can support you!" That's what I felt and said to myself at four o'clock in the morning in my restless review of the encounter.

You guessed it. I had to seek out the woman and

make restitution. After apologizing for my quick, angry retort, I opened the conversation about really trusting the Lord. And the apology opened the way for deep sharing. What I suspected was true; she had projected onto me her own need. Our conversation led to prayer and we were both helped.

James's admonition to be "slow to speak" not only is wise, but it also saves us a lot of time. If you're like me, you spend a lot of time and energy going back to mend relationships you have strained by unguided responses made too quickly, without waiting to hear the Lord's attitude and truth.

So often I hear people say, "I spoke without thinking." I've found that once the cycle of thought, emotion, and boiling blood takes place, I'd better wait before I speak. An even better method is to say nothing until the Lord has given us His thought and reaction.

All this helps us to understand James's admonition to be "slow to wrath," as the KJV words it. The Greek word for "wrath," also "anger," is *orgē,* meaning smoldring anger rooted in the fires of ego needs. James does not mean by slowness that we should put off expressing our anger creatively. What is implied is a period of prayer before we express our feelings.

The important thing in the handling of stress is that we allow our Christ-anointed thinking process to filter out what is unworthy of developing an agitated reaction in our nervous system and blood. We can ask, "Is this important enough to generate this much stress?"

And before the stress syndrome begins, we can allow Him to take charge of our feelings and our response. Often the person who has made us angry, or the situation which has caused an angry response, needs His love more than we need what we feel has been denied us.

James goes on to say, "For the wrath [anger] of man does not produce [or work] the righteousness of God" (v. 20). The righteousness of God, as it is used in Scripture, is right action in obedience to God, and what He has revealed as the way to live in response to His love. In other words, righteousness is rightness with God. It is through faith that we have been made right with God. And that same faith trusts Him to guide us in expressing our anger in a way that is creative for all who are involved.

In every situation that causes us anger, we need to ask the question: how can I deal with this conflict, this disagreement, this disappointment, this frustration, in a way that brings me closer to the living God and brings my relationships with others under His control?

Remember, we are responsible for what we say and what we do. Anything that does not deepen a relationship is sin, for sin is separation. Any action that makes us feel guilty in the presence of God and therefore feel fragmented from Him, is sin. The Greek for sin is *hamartia*, to "miss the mark," and any anger that forces us to miss the mark is sin. So the question is:

how do we allow God to take the things that distress us and then work them through our system so that we are able to respond with His love, His firmness, His forgiveness, and His abiding care?

The Apostle Paul helps us at this point as he quotes from Psalm 104 in Ephesians, " 'Be angry, and do not sin': do not let the sun go down on your wrath, nor give place to the devil" (Eph. 4:26–27). Or, as *The Living Bible* puts it, "Don't give the devil a beach-head." I like that. Often the unbridled expression of our anger breaks relationships and causes distress and confusion in the lives of other people. It does not bring them to a realization of how much God loves them or we love them.

I believe it is also important to realize that we have to earn the right to be angry creatively. It means that we have developed the quality of relationship with people so that they know we are for them regardless and that we'll stay with them through the difficulty. And then, in that context, we can say, "Let me tell you how I feel."

It is important, too, in expressing our feelings that we avoid any tone or note of condemnation. In other words, we have the right to tell a person how we are feeling, provided that we can do so without causing him or her to feel personally rejected. That can come only in the total context of facial, physical, verbal, empathetical listening and caring for him or her. Once we have established that kind of relationship with a person, we can say, "Bob, let me tell you how I felt the other day when you said—" Or, "Janice, please let me tell you how I felt when that happened." Or, "Let me give you my perception of what was going on." This kind of approach lets the other person know that what is said comes through a channel of love and acceptance, and he or she can receive it in that context.

Now how can we do that? Again, we get our guidance from James. He says we are to "receive with meekness the implanted word." The Greek word translated as "meekness" here is a many-faceted word which our contemporary understanding of meekness misses. For the Greek it meant the mean between excessive anger and no anger, implying a quality of control over the feelings and emotions. Aristotle used the word to mean moderation in the expression of anger, in which reason controlled expression and serenity was never lost. "Teachableness, receptivity to learning," was another dimension of the meaning of the Greek word. It might also be used in describing an animal that had been broken and could respond to the reins of its master.

All of these dimensions of the word contribute to our understanding of stress management. Meekness in the deeper meaning, then, describes a receptive, teachable, leadable mind that is in control of the expression of the emotion of anger.

How does that happen? Through the "implanted word" James talks about. "Implanted," *emphutos*, in

Greek refers to that which is inborn, innate to human nature, or it can mean that which is instilled or inculcated. Clearly James meant the latter because he says that we are to receive the word with meekness. When the idea of "implanted" is combined with "word," it means truth that is ingrained, ingrafted, in the tissues of our mind, in our cerebral cortex, as a result of conversion and the infilling of Christ's Spirit.

That's very exciting! If Christ lives in us, His mind and His attitude control and condition not only our needs but the reaction to the frustration of those needs. In this way Christ acts as a lightning rod within us. He takes the disturbing things that are said or done to us that would cause us anger and grounds them of destructive power over us. We react with His truth about reality and with His attitude about rejection or hostility. Before the anger signal is given to the limbic system, He intersects the process. It is as if He breaks the circuit which sounds "red alert" before it rings and flashes. Instead we are given His perception and grace in our response, and He responds through us!

The "implanted word" is another way of talking about the innate nature of a Christian. We receive a new nature when we come to be in Christ. We begin to live a Christ-filled life in which He is the source of the direction of our thought, our action and reaction. We begin to have His nature. And under the Master's direction, we become active in bringing justice not just in angry pronouncements or aloof indignation but in costly involvement, putting our time, energy, and money on the line. We become indignant at sin and the rules and regulations of religion that keep us from caring about people.

Instead of expressing destructive anger, we become involved to bring change. In our relationships with individuals, we are able to use the overflow of the abundant love He has given us through the indwelling of His Spirit. This love guides the expression of our concerns, and compassion enables us to express anger in a way that does not break our relationship with God or with other people. And we feel deeply in reaction to anything in society that dehumanizes or debilitates human beings.

We are indeed wondrously made. We belong to the Lord. When we allow Him to guide the formation and resolution of our anger, our body and mind function together to give our response a total impact not of hostility or hatred, but rather forgiveness and acceptance coupled with honesty and directness. This does not break relationships; it builds them.

As sons and daughters of our wonderful Lord, we can enjoy this kind of relationship with others as we pray with Whittier:

> Drop Thy still dews of quietness,
>   Till all our strivings cease;
> Take from our souls the *strain and stress*,
>   And let our ordered lives confess
> The beauty of Thy peace.*

* "Dear Lord and Father of Mankind," by John G. Whittier, 1872.

CHAPTER THREE

THE STRESS OF WHAT
~~~~~ ~~~~~
WE DO NOT EXPRESS

I really like the idea of not sweating the small stuff. So often we get distressed over little things that don't matter. But is all that causes us stress small stuff? What about the needs of people, the problems we could help solve, and the tense relationships between people in which we might become reconcilers? And in the more complex frustrations, are there really only three alternatives—to fight, flee, or flow?

A MAN LEFT CHURCH WITH A PARTING SHOT I'LL never forget. He looked me in the eye and said, "Your sermon this morning caused me a great deal of stress. I think that's because I didn't do anything about the message you preached last Sunday!" We both laughed.

"What about this week?" I asked. His response was, "I know what I have to do. The stress build-up last week because I didn't do anything about it has really gotten to me. I'll report in next week. Thanks for holding me accountable."

Later in the day I reflected on that statement. As I thought back to the sermon I'd preached the week before, I remembered that it had been on doing what love demands. I'd asked the congregation to focus on the people, problems, and challenges that needed their expression of love, forgiveness, or practical help, and to consider their calling to become involved.

The following week my friend did report in on what he'd done. He told me about the marriage difficulties with which he'd lived for years. His problem was that he could not express to his wife in words his affection for her. He had been raised in a family that never expressed affection or affirmation out loud. His wife had reminded him that she could count on her fingers the number of times he'd ever said, "I love you!" But he still couldn't or wouldn't do anything to change. Because of this long-standing unfilled need for affirmation and assurance, my friend's wife had become deeply depressed, and eventually she had cut off all sexual intimacy with her husband. The stress build-up caused in both of them was excruciating, and affected their entire family and his work. So, when he heard my sermon on the demands of love in our relationships, he had determined to talk his problem out with his wife and work at changing his ways. But then he put it off, and the guilt build-up was even greater.

After the sermon and our brief conversation on the second Sunday, he had gone home determined to do what was right. In the conversation that followed, he told her for the first time that as a boy he had never been told by his parents that they loved him or were proud of him, and because of this there was a great lack in his own life. He then asked her to forgive him for his neglect and told her he was determined to change. In the days that followed he consciously worked at regularly verbalizing his love for his wife. Later, when he reported progress to me, there was a broad smile on his face as he told me about their fresh and loving relationship and how the crippling stress that had so marred their marriage had all but disappeared.

There *is* a stress that builds up from what we do not express. Up to this point we've discussed the stress produced by anger over our frustration of not having *our* needs met. Now let's examine the stress we experience when we are confronted with other people's needs and for whatever reason put off doing or saying what love requires. It happens to us in marriage, in the family, among our friends, in difficult relationships where we work, and in problems that demand our attention.

There is a stress that develops in us when we feel impotent to do anything about seemingly impossible people and insolvable problems. But equally distressing is the guilt we feel because we put off doing what we know we should do and say to heal relationships and solve our problems. Most of us have experienced the haunting unrest and inner turmoil that comes with realizing that we have failed to properly express our feelings of love or appreciation or affirmation to family and friends.

Much is said and written about the stress produced in us by the blaring reports in newspapers and on television of all the complex problems, suffering, and violence in the world around us. As we read and listen to the horrible reports of war, terrorism, hunger, hopelessness, and suicide that keep our society in turmoil, we can feel the tension build. Stomach and shoulder muscles knot as the paralyzing poison of fear and hopelessness surges through us. On one hand we feel frustrated over events we can't change, and on the other hand we so often fail to make the needed changes in our own lives and relationships that would contribute to easing stress. In fact, I believe that the people who worry most over the complex problems in the larger world they cannot change are usually putting off acting redemptively to change what they can in their own small worlds.

Recently, cardiologist Robert Eliot of the University of Nebraska gave some advice about how to cope with stress that is being widely quoted. "Rule number one is, don't sweat the small stuff. Rule number two is, it is all small stuff. And if you can't fight or flee, flow."

I really like the idea of not sweating the small stuff. So often we get distressed over little things that don't matter. But is all that causes us stress small stuff? What about the needs of people, the problems we could help solve, and the tense relationships between people in which we might become reconcilers? And in the more complex frustrations, are there really only three alternatives—to fight, flee, or flow? Definitely not. There's another—discovering the loving, forgiving, reconciling, or transforming thing God wants to perform in and through us and others and cooperating with Him in making it happen. However, if by "flow" we mean seeking God's guidance and power and being carried by the fast-moving currents of His Spirit, then it can be a consistent release of stress. However, if "flow" means doing nothing, then it is quite likely we merely contribute to the stress-producing problems that affect us and others. Let's not allow the fact that there are many situations in which we cannot do or say anything helpful to keep us from acting and speaking when God can make a difference through us.

The Lord has made us a lot tougher than many of us imagine. He not only gave us a stress coping mechanism but a creative eustress-producing system that can provide us the stimulation to act and speak in response to His guidance. Often our stress over the "small stuff" of life is released when we get involved in healing problems and people—the "big stuff" of life.

We were programmed to be a riverbed for the flow of the Spirit of Christ. Inflow and outflow must be perfectly matched. Hearing about the love of Christ without being a lover of people will cause stress. We will be filled with distress when we are forgiven, but do not forgive. Faith without works of love will soon become a dead religious ritual. There is no stress in comparison to the stress of unexpressed good intentions. Guilt results. The distress of knowing what we should do and not doing it produces spiritual and emotional sickness.

At the same time, there's a great difference between the stress of true and false guilt. False guilt is what we continue to feel after we've been forgiven for what we've done; true guilt is what we feel when the Lord reminds us of what we should have done or need to do. One is guilt over what we've been; the other is guilt over what we refuse to be and do. For both, God offers stress-releasing forgiveness and reconciliation. And the sure sign that we've accepted His love will be that we act on His guidance for what we are to do in the future.

Once again our biblical writer speaks to our need. James knew the necessity of keeping faith and works together. From the end of the first chapter through the end of the second chapter, he emphasizes the importance of hearing and doing as equal parts of a balanced, healthy life. As children of God we are participants in a new humanity, and the Word will provide guidance for our actions and signals to our body systems that enable us to be implementers. We have been given the Lord's perspective to be able to see into people and situations with x-ray vision and discernment, knowing exactly what needs to be said or done.

But to fail to respond clogs up the channel and causes inordinate stress within us. It is disastrous to separate hearing from doing, believing from living, grace from caring and faith from works. James says, "Be doers of the word, and not hearers only, deceiving yourselves" (1:22, RSV); "So faith by itself, if it does not have works, is dead" (2:17, RSV).

That crucial advice for stress management is driven home with a powerful parable. James says that anyone who is a hearer and not a doer is like a man who observes his natural face in a mirror, "For he observes himself, goes away, and immediately forgets what kind of man he was. But he who looks into the perfect law of liberty and continues in it, and is not a forgetful hearer but a doer of the word, this one will be blessed in what he does" (1:24–25).

Here James reminds us of the power of positive imagination. We become the person we picture ourselves to be. Contemplation of what we've been perpetuates the pattern of the past. But a vivid image of the person the Lord wants to set us free to be enables us to press forward to becoming that person with His help.

Now, let's apply this principle of "hearing but not doing" to how stress builds up from what we do not express. If we picture ourselves as persons who know what we should do but who refuse to do it, that is precisely the way we will act. On the other hand, if we picture ourselves as eager receivers of the insight God wants to give us and who act in accordance with the truth as we understand it, our lives will be dramatically changed, and we will fulfill the picture.

For example, a friend of mine said, "Lloyd, I have discovered what causes me so much stress. I am troubled by the fact that I'm helpless to do anything about it. I make grand resolutions but one day of failure in implementing them is followed by another. Fear of failure keeps me locked into repeating the failures. That's been my problem all my life . . . guess it will always be that way." This man is holding a negative image of himself. He sees himself as a person who makes promises to himself, but even as he makes them, he knows that he won't follow through. What a sad misuse of creative imagination!

A young woman friend of mine is just the opposite. She has discovered that asking the Lord for guidance and then picturing herself as doing what He says to do has erased the negative image she had had of herself. She shared the secret with me. "In the morning I pray that the Lord will show me what I am to do and say, then I meditate on the picture of myself really doing and saying what He has shown me. I hold the picture in my mind all day. The amazing thing is that so often the picture becomes a reality."

These two people are late twentieth century examples of what James is talking about. *Constantly looking at the immobilized person we've been, unable to express love in action and words, is a sure way of remaining that way the rest of our lives.* Conversely, picturing ourselves as liberated persons marshals all our energies plus the power of the Lord's Spirit to accomplish the vision.

The gifts of imagination and will enable us to form, hold, and achieve the Lord's picture of us as people who hear His guidance and respond with obedience. The words James uses, "looking into the perfect law of liberty," give us the liberating secret. Let's consider what that means for us today. The word "perfect" in Greek means that which fulfills its purpose, end, or goal. "Law" means commandment, in the biblical sense—an admonition of law to live out the implications of our covenant relationship with the Lord. "Liberty" is the freedom to love the Lord, others, and ourselves. In that light, the perfect law of liberty is the love-motivated life, free of self-condemnation, constriction, and confinement.

Freedom comes from knowing that we are loved profoundly. Christ has reconciled us by setting us free of sin, fear, the need to justify ourselves, and the pattern of self-condemnation. He promised, "You shall know the truth and the truth shall make you free. . . . If the Son makes you free, you shall be free indeed" (John 8:32, 36).

What is the truth that sets us free? It is Christ Himself and what He revealed in His life, message, death, resurrection, and indwelling power. He is the heart of God with us with unmerited love, unreserved forgiveness, unlimited power, and unrestrained hope. Through the atonement of Calvary, we have been completely exonerated and declared "not guilty." The door on our past sins and failures has been closed. The future is open with immense possibilities.

How can we thank Him for what He has done? We do that by allowing Him to transform our thinking so that we can accept His truth as the basis of our eternal status as loved and forgiven people. He gives us the picture of what we are as free people. And the result is that imagination and will are brought into harmony. We are able to receive and implement His guidance. The deeper our relationship is in Him, the more His freedom becomes ours. Actually, we become like our Lord. He provides the picture of the unique, special miracle He intends us to be, He motivates us with His healing love, and He releases us to desire to know and do His will.

In your mind's eye, picture your life free of un-healed memories of all that you have done or failed to do. See yourself as a person free of compulsion, fear, and anxiety. Next imagine your body liberated from jangling tension inside. Feel the unified working of your whole nature to think the Lord's thoughts and act as an agent of communicating His love. Think about how you would react to stressful situations and people if you really believed the Lord were there with you to provide exactly what you need. Now hold that picture and constantly thank the Lord that He will make it possible. The amazing truth is that He wants that even more than we do.

In my own pilgrimage in discovering how to manage stress this picture of daily, hourly, imaginative prayer has transformed my life. As I begin each day, I try to picture each challenge and opportunity that will come in that day. I picture the Lord present in power, filling me with His wisdom and love. The brain has great power to form, hold, and marshal all our faculties to achieve the positive images we form. Paul said, "Now the Lord is the Spirit; and where the Spirit of the Lord is, there is liberty" (2 Cor. 3:17). We have liberty because we do not need to worry about being adequate. The Lord will supply all that we need to live through the day without excessive, debilitating stress. Knowing the future, He will prepare us with thoughts and experiences that can be called on in any moment of crisis or opportunity.

I believe that it is the dichotomy between faith and works that causes the guilt-stress syndrome in so many of us. And the reason for it is that we are really unsure that the Lord will intervene to help us. We fail to do what He wants because we are afraid we won't have what it takes. On that we are right. We don't—on our own. Stress develops when we try to live a responsible life on our own strength.

But the Lord did not create us to do His work on our own energy and cleverness alone. I tried that for years and ran out of steam. I would have to get "up" for each sermon, challenge, or demanding relationship. "Red alert" was flashing most of the time as my body systems struggled to keep pace. But when I was forced to see what this stress was doing to my body, I discovered the secret of living the supernatural quality of life I described earlier: Christ's Spirit controlling the cortex, fully releasing my intellectual potential, signaling the limbic system for the release of the needed energy, and then multiplying my resources with His unlimited power. I discovered that I could trust Him to go before me and prepare each situation and person with whom I would deal. He was with me, guiding my thoughts and reactions. He opened doors that previously were closed, and arranged possibilities I had not dreamed were possible. That broke the stress syndrome in which I had been living.

James, in his little book, gives us an intensely practical application of this truth. He is concerned about the attitudes of early Christians toward the economically and spiritually poor among them. Now you may wonder what that has to say about stress. I believe it has a great deal to say about it, for it brings us back to the central theme of this chapter. The stress we wrestle with in the world around us is directly related to the problems of the poor in body and in spirit.

We, you and I, have been entrusted with physical and spiritual wealth, but if we refuse to be involved in meeting the needs of the physically and spiritually poor, we will feel profound stress because we are denying the Lord's plan and contradicting His Spirit of love within us. The needs of people cry out for our help. It is true that we can't do everything, but to do nothing is to become spiritually sick.

Who are the poor in our lives today? The obvious answer even in today's world is—they are the economically, physically, or socially disadvantaged, which means that if we are to interpret the word of

James correctly, we must become involved in some specific program or activity that seeks to alleviate human need and suffering. All of the spiritually dynamic people I know have a social service dimension to their lives. They give a portion of their income to feed the hungry, and they devote time to working in a social program in their community. Faith without works of practical ministry for the poor and disadvantaged is not only dead, but dangerous to our spiritual health.

Recently a couple came to see me about the problem of stress in their lives and marriage. They were a comfortably settled, financially secure couple. Both were practicing, praying, and participating members of the church. The husband was feeling the strain of stress at work, and the wife was concerned about her health problems, which, according to her doctor, were caused by inner stress. We had several visits in which I listened to their needs and in which I shared some of the insights about stress that I was discovering in my own life. During one of these times together I shared with them my feelings about the stress we have because of what we fail to express. We talked about the people in their lives who needed their love and actions of concern. And they agreed that they had never thought of stress as being caused by their unwillingness to be involved with and to care about others. There was a complete absence in their lives of any effort to communicate Christ's love to others. The conversation ended abruptly, but the point had been made.

The next day the wife called and said, "Listen, Lloyd, we were so upset after yesterday's visit that we couldn't sleep. After tossing and turning for awhile, we finally got up and talked until dawn. We suddenly realized how irrelevant and uncaring and inconsistent our lives are. We spend more money on clothing, hairdressers, and dinners out than we give to the church. Both of us were alarmed to discover that our vacations cost more than we've ever given to any organization working with world hunger. And along with all of that we realized that our friends never call us when they are in trouble. I guess we're not the kind of people others feel they can talk to when things go bump.

"We wonder if our privacy about our own problems has caused that. We pretend we're always on top. So when you asked us if we'd ever talked to anybody about our faith, we were very disturbed. We don't even talk about our faith with each other, let alone with anybody else. This idea of the stress of what we do not express really hit us. We want to talk with you again and do something about our self-centered lives."

When we got together a few days later, they were ready to do some hard thinking. First, we talked about their own relationship. They had pretended to have the best marriage in California, but actually they were both very lonely because of the lack of deep sharing with each other. I suggested that if they would allow

God to meet their deep, inner needs, then do and say the affirming thing for each other, it would be a profound expression of love that would ease their loneliness. Next we talked about the importance of a daily devotional time together. I suggested a program called "Fifteen Minutes to Freedom," with five minutes for prayers of thanksgiving and praise for God's love and blessings, five minutes for reading the Bible, and five minutes for prayers of intercession and supplication. Then I told them about a small group of couples who met together regularly to discuss coping with stress, and I offered to introduce them to the group and help them become active participants.

Then we got down to financial specifics. We talked about tithing and the joy of giving. We discussed particular needs to which they could give gifts of money to alleviate hunger and suffering. But I emphasized the idea that giving money could not be a substitute for personal ministry.

They responded eagerly to all that we talked about. So in the days and weeks that followed they became involved with a group that was working to alleviate poverty in Los Angeles. The husband had leadership skills and business acumen badly needed by the organization, and the wife became involved in teaching reading and writing. Personal involvement soon opened their hearts to give more freely of their income. At the same time, they entered into an experiment of praying daily to be guided into situations and to people in need, and they committed themselves to "Fifteen Minutes to Freedom."

All this eventually brought the couple to the realization that they needed deeper understanding of their faith and how to share it with others. So, in addition to meeting with a small group, they became part of an in-depth study of the Bible offered by our church.

The significant thing is that this couple now have more people they are trying to help than do many professionals. And stress is no longer the besetting problem it had been because their past stress had been caused by what they had not expressed—either to the poor in an impoverished neighborhood, or to their friends in the executive suite of the man's company and in the country club in which they remained with the specific purpose of caring for the spiritually "poor" among the up-and-outers.

None of us has to look far to find the spiritually and emotionally impoverished "poor" in our own lives. They are in our families and among our friends; we work with or for them and they work for or with us. And often they are people who cause stress in our lives because of the stress in their own. When we make them a subject of prayer, seeking the Lord's guidance on what we need to say or do, He will give us marching orders.

Jesus put a great emphasis on hearing and doing. He knew that we were made to be persons for others.

He also observed that religion that is irrelevant to the needs of people is dangerous. It becomes a substitute for the Lord Himself. For example, Jesus saw the stress in the lives of the Pharisees who cared more for regulations than for people. He felt profound compassion for the rich young ruler whose stress was intensified by his desire to become His disciple but was unwilling to part with his wealth. At one point Jesus told His followers that to hear and not obey was like building a house on sand. And following His crucifixion Jesus visited with Peter by the Sea of Galilee to help him see the secret of overcoming the stress of his guilt for having denied Him. Peter's love for the Lord would have to be expressed in caring for people: "Feed my sheep."

All this becomes very personal for us. Who in our lives needs love, affirmation, and costly care? Where are we involved with the Lord in ministering to the "poor" in body, mind, or spirit?

So many of the analysts of stress tell us that we must learn to relax, slow down, retreat from conflict and tension. But Jesus says, in so many words, "Follow Me! We've got a world to change, people to love, situations to transform." From this we learn that losing our lives for Him and for the needs of people turns the pent-up stress into joy of service.

CHAPTER FOUR

HEART YOUR
TONGUE!

Most people are far more sensitive than we suspect. All of us are more sensitive than we would like to admit. And everyone lives in a world of insensitive people with undisciplined tongues.

I HAVE A DELIGHTFUL OLD SCOTS FRIEND WHO has a fascinating way of warning people about the careless use of their words. "Heart your tongue!" he says when he overhears anyone using words to demean, destroy, or debilitate others. This is his rendition of the more familiar phrase, "Mind your tongue!" He is using heart in the inclusive biblical sense of mind, emotion, and will. Years of experience have taught him that it is what's in the heart that produces what's on the tongue.

The purpose of this chapter is to focus on the uncreative stress caused by what we say to one another. The tongue has a mighty power to cause distress or eustress. Our words can discourage or encourage, burden or boost, agitate or affirm, tear down or build up, imprison with guilt or release with freedom, communicate condemnation or infuse self-esteem, express love or hate. The difference will be in the extent that we have been able to "heart our tongues"; to bring them under the thought-control that motivates loving emotion and the will to use them to set people free to fulfill all the potential of their gifts.

We turn again to the Book of James as a manual for stress management. The entire third chapter deals with the destructive and creative use of the tongue. James shows us the awesome power of the tongue and then the power of an awesome tongue.

The tongue and the words it forms can be a dreaded instrument of destruction or a wonder-filled, disciplined instrument of praise for our Creator and our fellow-creatures. The difference will be determined by what's stored up in the cortex of our brains, what that signals to the limbic expression of emotion, and what the cerebrum wills to communicate.

James uses several metaphors to expose the uncontrolled tongue and to extol the controlled tongue. One of these becomes a fulcrum for us in our consideration of the positive and negative use of words either to create or to relieve stress. All of the other metaphors James uses can then be marshaled in support of his basic thrust.

James admonishes, "Look also at ships: although they are so large and are driven by fierce winds, they are turned by a very small rudder wherever the pilot desires. Even so the tongue is a little member and boasts great things" (James 3:4–5a). In this vivid use of parable, James speaks of the power of the tongue and the control of the tongue and pictures a huge ship being guided in its course by a comparatively small rudder. The point, however, is that the rudder is a neutral piece of equipment that must be moved by the pilot or captain of the ship. The rudder is not a bad rudder just because the ship drifts or veers off course. Rather, the problem is with the one who guides the rudder, either by hand in smaller craft, or, in the case of an ocean liner, through the complex mechanical system directed by the helmsman at the wheel under the commands of the captain of the ship.

The parable has much to say about our subject of stress. The words formed by our tongues, like the rudder, can keep us on or throw us off course as persons. They can cause distress or eustress. Distress comes from words that threaten, frighten, enrage, or frustrate us. The same tongue can form words that motivate love, instigate courage, and implement action. The tongue can hurt or heal. It can be used to gossip or to mediate grace. We've all been victims of words and victimized others with them. We've blessed and blasted with the same tongue.

The reason for this is that the Lord has made us with the capacity to hear as well as speak. Through the wonder of hearing, the sound of a word flows through the auditory nerve to the cortex of the brain while neural circuits are actuated in comprehension of the word. This takes place in split-second time. Depending on the meaning we impart to the word from our prior learning and experience, the auditory cortex actuates the appropriate response. A word of affection or encouragement or an impelling call to action for a good cause will incite the limbic system to provide appropriate energy and emotional response.

But the opposite is also true. Angry, hateful, condemnatory words will flood our blood with body chemicals that can cause us physical damage. Disturbing words trigger the same "red alert" as dangerous situations and circumstances. Our defense system leaps into action to cope with the impact of words from another's tongue.

Add to this whole process the brooding capacity of the memory capability of the human brain. The stimulating, distressful words agitate the cycle repeatedly, almost endlessly. We all have long memories and short tempers when it comes to remembering what people have said to hurt us. Days, months, sometimes years later, words carelessly or maliciously spoken rumble about in the circuits of our memories. A familiar face or circumstance brings back the emotions and the hormonal discharge as if they had just been said. Most people are far more sensitive than we suspect. All of us are more sensitive than we would like to admit. And everyone lives in a world of insensitive people with undisciplined tongues.

James is very apt in his own description of the anatomy of distress caused by the tongue. He didn't know such terms of anatomy as cortex, limbic system, or cerebrum, but he had his own way of metaphorically explaining what he observed. "The tongue is so set among our members that it defiles the whole body, and sets on fire the course of nature" (James 3:6).

The words "course of nature" may also be translated "wheel of nature." The old Greek word used for wheel, *trochos* comes from a root word meaning "to run," and implies the unending circle or round in our nature of the impact of the words of the tongue. We would call that the cycle of increasing stress—first, hearing, then understanding, alarm, agitation, and adaptation of the nervous system.

The use of the image of fire in the course of our nature is also on target. Words that arouse rage, anger, fear, jealousy, and envy do "burn us up." We say, "The words you said to me made my blood boil!" This is just another way of describing the distressed state of an overstimulated sympathetic system that has pumped an excessive amount of chemicals into the blood. We do get "hot under the collar," and all over, for that matter.

The same metaphor of fire is used by James when he talks about the extent of the damage of careless or condemnatory words. "The tongue is a fire," he says. "See how great a forest a little fire kindles" (3:5). A thoughtless word is like a little fire that spreads to consume miles of forest. The implication is that our words travel not only to distress the individual but to disturb thousands who repeat those words carelessly in gossip.

There is a poignant story of a young man in a village of the Scottish Highlands who learned too late the destructive power of words. Out of envy and jealousy he had committed the character assassination of another man in the village, passing on a defaming story based on unsubstantiated, deprecating gossip. Later, through a personal encounter with the man, he learned that the tale he had been telling was totally untrue. Unfortunately, the offended man was too hurt to accept an apology.

Stricken with grief and guilt, the young man went to the village dominie to confess his careless defamation of character and receive forgiveness. The wise old pastor was not a disseminator of cheap grace. He knew of the virulent poison that now flowed in the minds of the people in the village because of the gossip. Instead of assuring him of forgiveness, he told the young man to do a very strange thing.

"If you want forgiveness and peace with your conscience, you must fill a bag with feathers and go to every dooryard in the village and drop in each of them a feather." Astonished, but penitent, the young man did as he was told. When he returned to the dominie he announced that he had accomplished the assignment and asked if now he could be forgiven.

"Not yet!" said the pastor sternly. "Take up your bag, go the rounds again, and gather up every feather that you have dropped." "But," exclaimed the young man, "the winds have surely blown them away by this time. Who knows how far they have been carried!"

"Yes, my son," answered the discerning spiritual leader, "and so it is with gossip and slander. Words are easily spoken, but no matter how hard you try, you can never get them back again."

"Then what can I do?" was the urgent response.

"Repent that you have murdered a man's character with your tongue. Ask God to forgive you. Surrender your tongue to God. And ask Him to heal the insecurity which is causing your envy and jealousy."

The disturbing story unsettles us as we are reminded of the many times we may have caused distress in others. It also alarms us about the irretrievability of words once they are spoken. We cannot get off the hook by saying, "Well, you know me. I don't always say what I mean." Vituperation is a costly vice! Nor can we equivocate by saying we are not responsible for how others take what we say. Gossip, slander, or deprecation with words is not easily absolved or corrected.

> Boys, flying kites, haul in their white-winged birds,
> You can't do that when you're flying words.
> Thoughts, unexpressed, may sometimes fall back dead,
> But God Himself can't kill them once they're said. *

*Author unknown; quoted in *1000 Quotable Poems*, compiled by Thomas Curtis Clark and Esther A. Gillespie (Chicago, New York: Willet, Clark & Co.).

Jesus called His followers to let their yes be yes and their no, no. He wanted us to say what we mean and mean what we say. We all long to have truly reliable people in our lives who are honest with us about our needs and supportive of our strengths. Using words to manipulate response, gain control, or pit people against others causes stress.

We need to think of the kind of words that cause distress. What are the "click" words that set off a reaction in your nervous system and emotions? What clicks into motion the chain reaction of distress in you? What kinds of statements can inflame you into heated argument? What gossip about you causes the greatest stress? Whatever our answers, we can be sure others feel the same way.

What can we do to get control of our stress-producing tongues—tongues that are loose at both ends, that wag in cutting, distress-producing words as if they were not connected either to clear thought or to sensitivity? James says, "For every kind of beast and bird, of reptile and creature of the sea, is tamed and has been tamed by mankind. But no man can tame the tongue. It is an unruly evil, full of deadly poison" (James 3:7–8). Grim analysis! It needs to be balanced by a return to the metaphor of the rudder, the pilot and the course of the ship. That combined with what James goes on to say gives us more hope.

The metaphor of the pilot and the movement of the rudder encourages us with the truth that the pilot of our tongue is the heart. And in this context, "heart" is to be understood in its biblical meaning of combined intellect, emotion, and will. We have more control of the tongue than we may have assumed.

A brief review of the anatomy of speaking may be helpful. Thought in the cortex of the brain activates the twelfth cranial nerve, called the hypoglossal, the motor nerve of the tongue. The tongue moves with the signal of thought through the hypoglossal nerve, arising in the medulla oblongata, the base of the brain.

Let's experiment with that. First, wag or move your tongue. Now as a voluntary act, press wind up through your vocal cords. By a signal from the cortex, you have both sound and movement of the tongue. Now add to that the movement of the lips, and the tongue can form words. All of this is an act of the will. Nothing can be formed by the larynx and the tongue that has not first originated in your mind. Verbal capability is a product of the cortex, the emotions, and your conscious will. This certainly seems to indicate that the tongue is untamable only if the mind is uncontrollable.

Jesus was very clear about the interrelationship between what we say and what we think and feel. He put the responsibility not on the tongue as an independent member of the body, but as a reliable instrument of the mind.

James carries out the same thought. He follows the danger of the duplicity of the tongue to the obvious conclusion that the tongue is not the culprit after all, but the source of thought and emotion and will. Continuing to speak of the tongue, he says, "With it we bless our God and Father, and with it we curse men, who have been made in the similitude of God. Out of the same mouth proceed blessings and cursing. My brethren, these things ought not to be so. Does a spring send forth fresh water and bitter from the same opening? Can a fig tree, my brethren, bear olives, or a grapevine bear figs? Thus no spring can yield both salt water and fresh" (James 3:9–12).

This brings us back to the words of my Scots friend, "Heart your tongue!" And now we can ask ourselves, what needs to happen in our hearts so that what is sent to the tongue to articulate is creative and not distressful?

"The meekness of wisdom" is James's answer. No one can convert the heart except the Lord. And He does it by invasion of His own Spirit. Then what we say will be what He wants said through us.

> Thy heart must overflow
> If thou another's soul would'st reach;
> It takes an overflowing heart
> To give the lips full speech.
> *Horatius Bonar*

When the pilot of the mind controls the rudder and that pilot is receptive, open, and obedient to the Eternal Pilot, the indwelling Lord, our tongues and the words we speak *can* be controlled by His clear charts of wisdom.

But what is this wisdom? James tells us it does not come from us or from the prejudiced, sensual, and demonic world around us. If the only source of thought to control our tongue is human nature, we are in trouble and so are the people who suffer from our misguided or selfish words. "For where envy and self-seeking exist, confusion and every evil thing will be there" (James 3:16).

Real wisdom is a gift of Christ dwelling in us. It is His mind infused into our minds. James uses several key words to tell us the components of this implanted wisdom.

First of all, it is pure, unadulterated. The words mean that which a thing is in and of itself with no admixtures. A pure word is one that is clear, with no mixed motive.

Second, wise words are peaceable. They are meant to communicate peace and to enable peace between people and the Lord, between them and their own selves, and between them and others. Words that cause uncreative conflict, distrust, or an agitated, combative spirit are not to be used. What we say to people and about them to others is to bring reconciliation and not the distress of discord. That cuts down a lot of talk, doesn't it?

Third, our tongues are to be gentle and willing to yield. The word "gentle" comes from an old Greek adjective that means reasonable, fair, and equitable. Willingness to yield means easy to be entreated, approachable.

Our tongues and words must be surrendered. They need conversion! We are challenged to commit what we say to others to be a channel of the Lord's Spirit. I have known many people who became Christians who eventually were confronted by the need to yield the control of their tongues to the Lord. One man said, "I have become aware of the stress I produce by what I say and how I say it. That's got to go if I am to go on with the Lord!" Have you ever felt that? Have you ever done it?

Fourth, wise use of the tongue is "full of mercy and good fruits." Mercy produces good fruits in others. Our tongues can be instruments for expressing forgiveness, acceptance, assurance, and affirmation. That relieves distress and enables the eustress of creative desire in others to be all that the Lord intended them to be.

All of us are aware, of course, of just how far short we come of measuring up to what we should be. And our feelings of unworth and failure have frequently been fortified by what others have said about us. But we urgently need people who will sense what we've been through and lovingly help us to face life's demands—people with the sensitive capability of getting inside another person's skin to feel what she or he is feeling. "Walking in another person's shoes" usually gives us a totally new perspective and may well turn our criticisms into acceptance and affirmation.

Fifth, a wisdom-controlled mind issues in words which have no partiality. How often words are used to compare people with others. We make distress-producing comparisons that negate people's individuality. Then, too, in families or among our friends, our words betray a greater love or admiration for one over the other. We try to get people to change by telling them we wish they were like someone else we admire more. We often use words to choose up sides, to pit people against others. But a Christ-controlled mind sends signals to the tongue to enable people to be the special and unique persons they are.

Sixth, wisdom at the helm of the rudder of the tongue shuns hypocrisy. The word means "to play a part; to go double." It is to dissemble by being one thing in our minds and saying another thing with our mouths. Words, then, are used to hide our real feelings and thoughts. Honesty in our speech must be carefully blended with all the above five elements so that we can say exactly what is on our minds without destroying people. Honest words without mercy are brutality and mercy without honesty is sentimentality. When we truly love people and have earned the right through deep caring to share our thoughts and feelings with them, we will be heard, and eustress of good motivation for change will be produced rather than immobilizing distress.

It can happen! The Lord can control our tongues when we give Him our hearts. We don't need to cause distress by the misguided words we say. There does not need to be an endless succession of broken relationships, hurt people, and shattered lives because of our tongues. "Heart your tongue!"

Here's a prayer from an old hymn that I love to repeat when I want my tongue to be under the orders of the Captain of my soul.

> Lord, speak to me, that I may speak
>   In living echoes of Thy tone;
> As Thou hast sought, so let me seek
>   Thy erring children lost and lone.
> . . . .
> O teach me, Lord, that I may teach
>   The precious things Thou dost impart;
> And wing my words, that they may reach
>   The hidden depths of many a heart.
>
> O fill me with Thy fullness, Lord,
>   Until my very heart o'erflow
> In kindling thought and glowing word,
>   Thy love to tell, Thy praise to show.*

* "Lord, Speak to Me" by Frances Ridley Havergal, 1872.

CHAPTER FIVE

THE ANTIDOTE FOR
COMBATIVE COMPETITION

Competition isn't bad if it prompts us to pull out all the stops and live at our own full potential. But when it eats away at us, we begin to take our readings from other people rather than affirming ourselves as special and unique persons.

THERE'S AN ANCIENT GREEK LEGEND THAT ILLUS-trates beautifully the plight of combative competition. In one of the important races, a certain athlete ran well, but he still placed second. The crowd applauded the winner noisily, and after a time a statue was erected in his honor. But the one who had placed second came to think of himself as a loser. Corrosive envy ate away at him physically and emotionally, filling his body with stress. He could think of nothing else but his defeat and his lust to be number one, and he decided he had to destroy the statue that was a daily reminder of his lost glory.

A plan took shape in his mind, which he began cautiously to implement. Late each night, when everyone was sleeping, he went to the statue and chiseled at the base hoping so to weaken the foundation that eventually it would topple. One night, as he was chiseling away the sculpture in violent and envious anger, he went too far. The heavy marble statue teetered on its fragile base and crashed down on the disgruntled athlete. He died beneath the crushing weight of the marble replica of the one he had grown to hate. But in reality he had been dying long before, inch by inch, chisel blow by chisel blow. He was the victim of his own stressful, competitive envy.

The tragedy was that no one knew how envious he had been. He had covered up the war raging in the silence of his own bitterness. The sickness of envy was like a cancer in his soul. If the fallen statue had not done him in, the envy he felt would have done so.

We all have such feelings at times. Who can escape? It seems there is always someone who has more or can do better. Comparisons are not only odious, but debilitating. The rotting in our souls has a foul smell. Our criticism of people we envy is little different from the defeated athlete's chisel blows. We too cut away at the foundation of the lives of those we envy. But we are the ones who topple from our potential greatness as people.

One of the major causes of stress which we all feel inside is combative competition. A more accurate word for it is envy. It is rooted in a lack of self-esteem, grows in the soul-soil of comparisons, and blossoms in noxious thorns of desire for what others have or achieve. When we feel others excel beyond us, we get the same "red alert" reaction in our nervous system as is prompted by fear, pressure, cutting words, or loss. We become agitated by the accomplishments of others. The result in our bodies is very harmful and the expression in our attitudes is very destructive to our relationships. Envy and jealousy are sleepless bedfellows who keep each other awake day and night in their fitful agitation. And in turn their restlessness keeps us agitated, under stress.

Recently, an executive in a certain company was telling me about one of his employees. "If that guy ever stopped working so hard at pretending he's working, he'd get ahead. Problem is, he's always taking his own success pulse, comparing himself and his job with others. He's not a keen competitor, he's a combative competitor. He works so hard at looking great, he'll never be great. Truth is he doesn't need to pretend to compete. He's got what it takes. All he needs to do is affirm his own potential, stop worrying about what others do, and get moving."

I asked my friend if he'd ever said that to the younger man. He laughed and said, "No, I haven't. I know I should. But then, he'd probably get moving so fast he'd be in place for my job!"

Both men were suffering from envy. But the one who could so incisively analyze the other was not aware of his own.

There's always someone ahead of us on the fast track. But stress surges within us when we want to beat others rather than do our best. Competition isn't bad if it prompts us to pull out all the stops and live at our own full potential. But when it eats away at us, we begin to take our readings from other people rather than affirming ourselves as special and unique persons.

L. B. Flynn, in *You Can Live Above Envy*, puts it all too plainly: "The envious man feels others' fortunes are his misfortunes; their profit, his loss; their blessing, his bane; their health, his illness; their promotion, his demotion; their success, his failure."

It is this attitude that leads to negative criticism. There boils up within us something of the spirit of the rhyme. "I hate the guys who minimize and criticize the other guys whose enterprise has made them rise above the guys who criticize." We've all been both the critical and the criticized. Both cause excruciating stress, and the question we must ask ourselves is: what can we do about what that does to us and others?

For the answer we turn again to our stress management manual—the Book of James. It is amazing how up to date these words are. James saw envy and competition as a tragic threat to the early Christians, and he asked and answered a crucial question, "Where do wars and fights come from among you? Do they not come from your desires for pleasure that war in your members?" (4:1). The use of the word "members" does not refer to the congregation, but to the component parts of our character. He points out here that our goals are not matched by the performance of our lives. We are at war inside ourselves. We have seen the enemy and it is us, and others are victims of our inner unrest.

The word "pleasure" that James used in this verse does not mean just sensual or material lust. It refers also to the driving desire of our egos for recognition and success. What he is launching a full-scale attack against is the insecurity within our minds that forces us to take our value signals from a comparison of what others are and do.

There's no doubt about it—the curse of envious competition is a prime cause of stress. We've all experienced that insecurity that overwhelms us at times because someone else is outdoing us. We are spurred on in the race, not so much to reach the goals God has given us as to outdistance others. It is a no-win marathon against others—really against ourselves. Others must be pushed down or tripped in their running of the race of life in order for us to be out ahead.

Now, I hasten to say at this point that healthy competition in a sport or business is not bad. It can be a part of the fun of life—with wins and losses. Every great athlete and successful business person wins when the goal is to do his or her very best, not just to defeat another. In those high moments the purpose is not to defeat the competition but to produce at maximum. That may result in a better score or product or service than our competitors, but winning is living at our maximum, not minimizing the accomplishments of our competitors.

The focus of James's concern is what envious competition does to our relationships. It denies Christ's victory over sin and death by substituting our values for His. We keep running a race we've already won through Calvary. We take our readings from others rather than from Christ and His victory for all of us. The result is that we become silent antagonists of each other rather than enthusiastic members of each other's cheering section.

Thoughtless, insensitive comparison with others pits us against them, and we put them down in an effort to bolster ourselves. Cancerous criticism results. Unfortunately, this can happen in the church, which can then become a house of judgment instead of a fellowship of mutual esteem and encouragement. The peace and unity is replaced by strife and stress. Billy Graham was right. "Envy can ruin reputations, split churches, and cause murders. Envy can shrink our circle of friends, ruin our business, and dwarf our souls. . . . I have never seen a man who profited in any way by being envious of others, but I have seen hundreds cursed by it."*

The stress of envious competition has been around

---

*Billy Graham, *Seven Deadly Sins* (Grand Rapids, Mich.: Zondervan Publishing House, 1955), pp. 41–42.

for a long time. Cain murdered Abel because of it. Jacob's lack of self-esteem prompted him to envy Esau's relationship with their father Isaac. Joseph's brothers tried to murder him because of the virulent poison of their competition with him. Envy set Aaron against his brother Moses. Saul was a burning cauldron of envious instability because of David's victories. The disciples competed with one another for first place in Jesus' attention. Paul and Peter often were at odds and openly critical of each other. Christian history has been a despicable record of denominational strife. And even the most pious of Christians have consistently envied each other's spiritual growth or accomplishments. Envious competition is Satan's power tool to separate those who should be inseparable participants in the grace of Christ.

But, in penetrating fashion, James goes into the deeper cause of envy. He calls it lust for what we do not have. We covet the opportunities and skills of others, which seem to exceed our own. The cause is lack of self-esteem. We miss becoming the unique, special persons the Lord has created each of us to be. Comparisons, plus combative competition, equal the stress of envy.

The secret of managing that stress is to ask for the Lord's help—not just for strength to excel, but for that liberating sense of our own value. James says, "You do not have because you do not ask."

Ask for what? We are to ask for the Lord's goals for

us and the power to accomplish them. The Lord does not play favorites or pit us against one another. He is for us and not against us. We can ask Him, "Lord, who am I? What do You want me to do? What are Your resources to accomplish Your vision for my life?" Have you ever dared to ask that? It is the antidote to envy. To be the miracle God planned for us to be is the most demanding assignment of life. But we've not been asked to attempt it without His power.

James goes on to say that so often the problem with our prayers is that we set our own goals based on our own desires and then ask the Lord to pull them off for us. That causes us even greater stress. Not only are we in competition with other people, now we are in competition with Him for first place in our lives.

Then, too, we all wrestle with the stress of unanswered prayer. Often our prayers are not answered because they are not prayers, but demands for blessing to do what the Lord has not willed. Envy is cut at taproot when we confess to the Lord that we have taken our eyes off Him and His will and are experiencing the feeling of competing with others. He does not will failure. He is a God of the successful accomplishment of *His* plans. Our task is to get into line with His purposes for us; then there is unlimited power to accomplish them.

John gave the early church the secret of how to do that. He said, "And this is the confidence that we have in Him, that if we ask anything according to His will,

He hears us. And if we know that He hears us, whatever we ask, we know that we have the petitions that we have asked of Him" (John 5:14–15).

Note the progression: we ask for His will; then we make petitions in accordance with His will; only then do we have the confidence that we have received, even before we ask, the answers to the prayers that we pray. Prayer is not to get what we want when we want it; rather, it is conversation with God in which we receive clarification of what to ask for and boldness to dare to ask.

Recently I talked to a man who was very critical of a "friend." He cut him to pieces with harsh judgment. As we talked, I sensed that there was something more than righteous indignation. "Have you ever wished you were in this person's shoes? Ever wished you had his opportunities and challenges?" What followed was the flow of jealousy draining from the cesspool of envy.

The two men had been rivals for years. The other man always seemed to be out ahead. Life had been so much easier for him, my friend said. He never realized he was envious.

But it would have done no good to tell him to stop being envious. The causes were deeper in his own lack of self-affirmation. He was down on the other man because he was not up on himself. Until he discovered the unique wonder he was, he would always find a hate object for his uncomfortable lack of self-appreciation.

Mustering up my courage and drawing on my own experience, I said, "Until you let God love you profoundly—to the point of excitement over your uniqueness—you will shift this envy from one person to another. And there always will be someone who seems to have more than you." I could see I had touched a raw nerve. Blood rushed to his face. I dared to cause stress to help him find a cure for the stress of envy that was crippling him. "You will be envious of others until you get converted!" I went on.

The man was a Christian and didn't like that. As a matter of fact, he got very angry and wanted to close the conversation. "What do you mean?" he said with a tone of a wounded animal.

"The result of being loved by God is creative self-love," I responded. "Feeling good about ourselves is the sure sign that we have been converted from self-hate to creative self-appreciation. You are special and so is your friend. Love for him with all his hang-ups will flow out of the well of a new self-image. Ask God what He wants you to be and do. Get on with it. You are not racing against your friend but for God's goal."

It was a crucial time of confrontation. The gift of the Spirit of God in that moment resulted in an openness to what had been said. We prayed together, asking for the Lord's plan and strategy and for the power to sight on His destination and not on other people.

James goes on to focus on envy as the cause of our committing adultery with the world. The language is electric! When our desire for something or someone has become the competing loyalty which vies for our love for God, James warns that we are committing adultery with the world.

The images James uses are potent. The solution to our destructive jealousy of others is to experience the creative jealousy of God. That may startle us. And yet, the Scriptures are filled with the Lord's own words declaring His unwillingness to accept any place in our hearts except as Lord. The very nature of His lordship is that it cannot be shared with any other. He puts it plainly. "I am the Lord thy God, a jealous God" (Exod. 20:5). Having been married to God by His predestined choice, call, and commission to be His own, we belong first and only to Him. When we desire worldly goals more than we desire Him, we enter into a love relationship that competes with that primary relationship. We put success, recognition, and our desires above Him, and we become adulterous, idolators. We idolize the world's standards and thus are drawn into envious competition with others, with the result that we experience excruciating stress until we put God first in our lives and commit ourselves to do His will.

So, envy is really lack of self-appreciation. We miss the special, unique person each of us is. And we fail to understand how much Christ loves and cherishes us. When He takes up residence in us, our desire is to be the person He means us to be. We don't have to be like any other person, do what he or she does, or love what rightfully belongs to someone else. In reality combative competition is the result of our uneasy state of grace. We judge others to lift up ourselves. But our "put-downs" put down only one person—ourselves.

James advises us, "Humble yourselves in the sight of the Lord, and He will lift you up" (4:10). That means accepting ourselves as the special persons we are, for we can rest easy in the fact that the Lord will multiply our potential beyond our wildest imagination. An honest recognition of our assets and liabilities, multiplied by His indwelling power, will equal excellence without stress.

We don't have to be eaten alive by the stress of envious competition. The sure way to redirect the energy misused on comparisons is to become the leader of the cheering section of those whom we are tempted to envy. As we cheer for them, we will be set free. Boosting others will send us and them soaring beyond the capabilities we thought we had. The Lord wants us to be as delighted as He is with the special person in our skin!

Recently a golfing friend of mine presented me with a photograph that now hangs on a wall in my home where visitors are sure to notice it. It is a constant reminder that I can enjoy being myself—even as an amateur golfer. The picture is of a scoreboard at the completion of a professional golf tournament in which America's top golfers competed. My friend had altered the photograph and put my name in the place of Jack Nicklaus. No one believes it when they see it, but it sure starts some great conversations and a lot of fun. It helps me laugh at myself as a golfer when I tell people my score is usually twenty to thirty points over Nicklaus's sixty-eight!

Each day as I pass that photograph I am brought back to the absurdity and danger of thinking envious thoughts of others. The picture is so unbelievable it makes me realize that my challenge is to do the very best I can and enjoy being myself to the highest degree of excellence my potential multiplied by God's power can produce.

CHAPTER SIX

THE TRUTH
ABOUT BURNOUT

Some of us have the idea that our worth is related to how much we do. But we can never do enough to fill that bottomless pit of trying to earn our self-esteem. Then, some of us have the attitude that no one can do the job right except us. And the most defeating of all is trying to live on our own strength without allowing God to help us.

WE HEAR A LOT ABOUT BURNOUT THESE DAYS. It's defined as working too hard, too long, under too much pressure. The symptoms are fatigue, health problems, and lack of creativity. The result is that a person no longer can produce effectively and no longer enjoys what he or she is doing. The panic over this problem in industry, the medical profession, and among some marriage and family counselors has caused a scrambling for a quick and easy solution. "Do less!" is often the remedy offered.

You can relax. This chapter is not another guilt-producing "slow down or break down" tirade to add to the literature on stress. I've read enough of those and had more than enough sent to me to wallpaper my house. The "do less and live longer" nostrum is pre-scribed by friends, loved ones, and doctors as a simplistic cure-all. It doesn't work for everybody. In fact, I'm wondering if it works for anyone.

It's how we do what we do, not how much we do, that causes stress.

Living a full, fast-track life need not cause stress. Even an overloaded life with too much to do does not always produce stress. There are people who handle immense responsibilities at home, work, and in church and community activities and do them with amazing effectiveness and ease. They've learned how to employ their stress-coping mechanism to work for them, not against them.

The problem is not in how much we do but in the goals, attitudes, and resources with which we do it. Burnout really is caused by taking on too much for the wrong reasons. Being unable to say no may be caused by a deep insecurity and lack of clearly defined goals for life. Some of us have the idea that our worth is related to how much we do. But we can never do enough to fill that bottomless pit of trying to earn our self-esteem. Then, some of us have the attitude that no one can do the job right except us. And the most defeating of all is trying to live on our own strength without allowing God to help us.

Burnout is not limited to the executive suite. It happens to people at all levels of industry. Factory workers, secretaries, salespeople, and research scientists can all suffer the "what's the use!" emotional and physical fatigue.

It can happen to housewives in the responsibilities of marriage, family, and related community responsibilities. Suddenly life loses meaning and purpose, and the smallest tasks seem to have become a mountain of drudgery.

Increasingly burnout is happening among those who work with people—clergy, doctors, counselors, and social workers. The draining demands of people and their problems suddenly become too much. Knowing the vast number of people who are hurting and in need, and realizing the likelihood of never being finished, the healer is wounded with debilitating anxiety.

Then again, community social work has produced its own number of burned-out volunteers. A person can be working in many good causes and one day wake up to the realization that he or she has lost verve and vitality. "Why am I doing all this? Who cares as much as I do? Is what I'm doing making any difference? Whom am I trying to impress with all this? If I got sick and missed a dozen meetings, who would care?" These are the questions we ask when we lose track of why we are doing so much, when the results seem minimal. We want to fade into the masses of people in our communities who are uninvolved, don't care, and accept things as they are.

The church is not exempt from burnout. Church leaders and lay workers are feeling it increasingly. Working for God gives no sure exemption from exhaustion. Running a religious institution has its duties and responsibilities that require committees and organization that can become as draining as any other work.

Church work, when purpose and power is lacking, can become boring and burdensome. The problem is that it is more difficult to admit. It's not only letting yourself and others down; it seems like a denial of God. I meet these burned-out church people everywhere. Many had a vital experience of God and then got ground into the church organizational machinery and not only lost their enthusiasm for endless committee meetings, but also for any vital contact with the Lord of the church.

As one man said recently about his church in the Middle West, "I had to back off. Fussing with conflict between groups struggling for power in the church, raising budgets, and keeping the organization going, I lost the fire, the excitement, the joy of my faith. I lost track of why I was doing it all. There seemed to be a lack of adventure, of doing something we could not do without God's power. Why, I think He could withdraw His presence from my church and the people would not know it happened. Maybe He has. Oh, I go to worship, say my prayers, and try to live out my faith on my job and at home, but I'm tired of church work!" The man had done too much for too long, under too much pressure without clear goals and an adequate inflow of inspiration and strength.

Do you know the feeling? Have you ever felt that about your job, about marriage, or activities, or life as a whole? Who hasn't? What's the solution? For me, it's not just doing less, but doing the right things for the right reasons. It's having the freedom to say yes to some things and no to others because we have a clear understanding of our central goal. It's discovering that there is enough time and available spiritual power to do the things God wants us to do. And it's trusting God to control our thinking and attitudes to employ our stress coping mechanism to the maximum.

It's amazing that anyone living in A.D. 50 could have anything to say about burnout in the contemporary asphalt jungle. And yet James gives us the secret of living without the fear of burnout. In James 4:13–17, there are four keys for keeping life aflame—energy, enjoyment, enthusiasm, and excitement.

James is as up to date as this morning's newspaper in the way he describes the blessing of life, the bane of the wrong attitudes about life, the brevity of life, and the potential beauty of life.

James was writing to the Hebrew Christians some of whom were itinerant merchants. He wanted to help them keep their faith aflame. Their problem, like ours, was that they were developing their life, their movements from city to city, and their involvements, without seeking and doing the Lord's will. They were still in charge of their own lives even after becoming Christians. A vital part of their gifts had not been committed to the Lord. The volitional power of the will was still under their own control.

Note what James has to say, "Come now, you who say, 'Today or tomorrow we will go to such and such a city, spend a year there, buy and sell, and make a profit'; whereas you do not know what will happen tomorrow. For what is your life? It is even a vapor that appears for a little time and then vanishes away. Instead you ought to say, 'If the Lord wills, we shall live and do this or that.' But now you boast in your arrogance. All such boasting is evil. Therefore, to him who knows to do good and does not do it, to him it is sin" (James 4:13–17).

The endowed capacity of will is a blessing of God for our life. The volitional portion of our brain creates a vital link between the thinking cerebral cortex and the drives of the limbic system. The will was meant to be the servant of our thinking. It was intended to take what we decide we want in an opportunity, task, or challenge, and energize the limbic system in providing the release of the hormonal resources to act.

James is awed by the sheer wonder of the blessing of the fact that you and I have the volitional capacity to choose, to decide, to declare the direction and destiny of our lives. In so speaking, he comes to grips with the wonder of free will, God's most gracious gift next to salvation itself, so that we can choose to believe that what He did in Jesus Christ was for us so that we might live now and forever.

But we can also say no. We have a free will. It is a part of the blessing of life. The Lord has not made us as marionettes or puppets. He does not coerce us. He will not bypass the picket line of a resistant will. He works within us to make us eager to be willing to desire to do His will.

A rebellious or uncooperative will can cause us no small amount of difficulty and tension, simply because of our failure to follow through and do what we should. We've all known times when we wanted to do or say something and were held back by a mysterious force within us. The will was debilitating instead of implementing our thought. Paul expressed this when he wrote, "For the good that I will to do, I do not do; but the evil I will not to do, that I practice" (Rom. 7:19). In late twentieth century language, this is what I think he is saying: "I think what is good but my will does not follow through in implementing it through signals to the nervous system controlling action and the energy needed to do it." When there is internal conflict caused by unclear direction of thought, we will do some things we do not really want to do and fail to do other things we wanted to do.

The conversion of the will is vital to a liberating experience of grace. Luther spoke of the bondage of the will, referring to the truth that we don't naturally want to do God's will. But the surrender of the will is essential to having our nervous system function properly. Otherwise we will have a battle of will with God which puts our minds and bodies into stress spasms. I think this is a major cause of burnout. Not doing too much, but being unsure of what we really want to do, doing things we don't want to do, and not doing other things we really want to do. The will was meant to be the implementer, not the impeder of thought.

So, James asserts the blessing of being able to will, but at the same time he alerts the early Christians to the truth that unless their wills were brought under submission to the "implanted word" in the cerebral cortex, the thinking brain, they would continue to make improper choices. James talks forcefully to those Christians whose experience of salvation had not brought them under daily guidance by the indwelling mind of Christ. When James says, "You do not know what will happen tomorrow," he is really saying, "You haven't asked the Lord what He wants for your tomorrow." They were missing the joy and peace of trusting the Lord.

In a positive way, let me describe what I think the Lord wants for us. He loves us and wants us to want what He wills for us. Since He is for us and not against us, He wants to guide our decisions so they will be best for us in the accomplishment of His will. He wants us to receive His love, abide in Him, and live a creative, productive life of glorifying Him and enjoying Him in all of life. At the same time, He will not lead us into any decision, relationship, job, or opportunity which will hinder our primary relationship with Him and His plan for us.

But if our wills are not surrendered to Him, we will make choices that defeat us. We will also be prompted by insecurity or self-aggrandizement into taking on tasks that make it difficult to do the things He really wants us to do.

The Lord knows us better than we know ourselves. And He wants to help us understand who we are and where we are going. Then when we ask His help in shaping these, He does a mysterious, wonderful thing. He guides our thinking and our surrendered wills. The more we grow in fellowship with Him, the more we can trust ourselves to want the right things. We can know that if we want to do something, and it does not deny our relationship with Him, or His purpose for us to seek first the kingdom of God, or the Ten Commandments, we can do it with delight.

I talk to people all the time who are running out of fuel because they loaded their lives down with things they didn't really want to do. People do not burn out from doing too much of what they delight in doing! Actually it's doing too much that denies what we really want to do.

I am constantly amazed, though, at how few people really know what they want out of life and how many fewer have ever asked the Lord to help them decide. They become victims of demanding schedules, people pressure, and debilitating stress. In fact, they victimize themselves, because they have no basis for saying yes or no to opportunities or responsibilities that come along. The result is that we get into things we think we have to do and expend a great deal of energy in the frustration of doing them.

I visited with an executive who was experiencing burnout. He had progressed successfully in his company, and his fellow employees considered him competent, efficient, and a team player. This brought him the recognition of his superiors who offered him opportunities to take on new projects. He enjoyed the challenge and took them on with gusto. But soon, handling his own job plus the added responsibilities began to wear on him. Instead of discussing the feeling of overload with his superiors and trusting them to balance his workload, he felt this would be an admission of weakness and failure. So, in order to get everything done, he began working late into the night. In fact, he seldom left for home before midnight, and before long he added Saturday and most of Sunday to his work schedule. The lack of rest and recreation made him less efficient and everything he did took longer. At the same time, he began to feel that he was the only one who really cared about what went on so he entrusted less and less to the people who worked for him. He became aloof and moody. Nothing people did for him pleased him.

You can imagine what that did to his marriage. His wife felt cut out of his life and their times together became less frequent. The man had little time for the recreational things they had enjoyed together. Time with his teenage children was cut to a minimum and they complained that even when he was with them he seemed distracted and impatient.

All this put my friend's nervous system into "red alert" twenty-four hours a day. He became like a battle weary soldier who had been in combat for years without relief.

You guessed it—he finally broke down. He suffered fatigue, then headaches, then ulcers, and finally a heart attack, which fortunately was severe enough to shock him, but not so critical as to disable him permanently.

After he had recovered from the heart attack he asked to meet me for lunch. Our conversation lasted through lunch and long into the afternoon. My friend was a Christian, but he had never thought much about allowing the Lord to guide his life. He wanted to know how to do that so he would not repeat what he'd been through. His life had gotten out of control, and he knew it.

In response to my question as to why he had taken on more than he could handle, he said it was because he wanted to succeed and get ahead. But on further reflection he identified a deep fear of failure. It was this that had kept him from asking for help from his superiors in having some of his duties assigned to others. Further reflection indicated that he had enjoyed his earlier duties, and the added tasks he took on led him into responsibilities for which he had little training or experience. So, not wanting to fail, he pretended he knew more than he did and worked extra time to cover up for his inability. Now everything became drudgery, and he became a driven man who lacked trust in the very people who could have helped him. He became a solo flyer and eventually crashed.

When we had talked through all that had happened, my friend was freed up to look at the future. "What do you want to do with the rest of your life?" I asked. He talked about what he enjoyed doing and fortunately there was such a job open. Then he admitted how much he really had missed time with his family and the days off and vacations that had been missed during the years of his compulsive race to escape "failure."

Most important of all, he wanted to get into a joyous relationship with God. He had not prayed consistently for years except when he felt the whirlpool sucking him deeper and deeper. Whatever else he did with the future, he wanted to get "right with God," as he put it, and to have time for him and his wife to be with other couples who were seeking to put God at the center of their lives. At the end of the conversation, we prayed together. I had explained the importance of not only believing in God, but surrendering our wills to Him so that He could help guide us. In one of the most honest prayers I ever heard, the man committed his future, asked for guidance, and opened his mind and heart, inviting the Lord to live in him.

In later visits, we worked on the clarification of his goals, the ingredients of a healthy life, and a balance of family, work, recreation, and times with other Christians to enrich his life. He and his wife became a part of a prayer and Bible study group of other executives and their wives. Together they sort out the Lord's will for their lives and support each other as they need, daring to say yes to some things and to say no to other things. Now he's on the way back to sanity.

The remarkable thing about this man's story is that he now realizes that getting sick was almost a conscious choice to escape the impossible life he'd taken on by a series of unguided choices. So often our bodies must bear the brunt of the stress that lack of clarity in our minds and wills produces.

Meanwhile, back to you and me. Are we clear about our goals? Have we asked for long-range direction and daily guidance? Are you enjoying your life? Is your work fun? How do you feel when you wake up to another day? Excited or burdened with the tasks ahead?

At a point in this past year I had an experience that alerted me to the first danger signs of burnout in my own life. I was racing across town to catch a plane for a speaking engagement. Suddenly I felt a resentment inside about having to make the trip. I wasn't looking forward to it at all. The fun was gone.

On the plane, instead of working, I leaned back to ask myself the questions I asked you in the paragraph above. Then I checked my date book. I realized that during the year I had been on a marathon travel schedule. Most of my speaking engagements are scheduled at least three years ahead, and I realized I had accepted dozens of them for this year without adequate prayer and without checking to see what came before and after each engagement. Why had I said yes to too many requests? And why, suddenly, was I feeling less than excited about this engagement and the heavy load ahead? After all, the Lord had always given me extra strength to pull off an impossibly heavy schedule!

As my plane sped across the country, I felt like Jonah heading for Tarshish instead of Nineveh. That caused me to ask, "How much do you enjoy doing? What's the number of engagements you can take and maintain priority time for your marriage, family, church, television ministry, and writing books?" I surrendered that decision to the Lord and asked Him to guide me to a solution.

The next day in my quiet time with the Lord I received the answer. It would be fun to take one major speaking engagement a month. A sense of relief came over me as I contemplated the relaxed joy of that kind of schedule. When I returned to my office, I reviewed the schedule prayerfully, cancelling those engagements that I could. Now in planning for years ahead, I know what I can accept in any one month.

The process wasn't easy, but the relief was delicious. I felt the Lord had stepped in to remind me that He was in charge. It would have been self-defeating to block His guidance. He had clarified priorities for me.

Life is short. We have such a few years to do the things the Lord wants each of us to do. To miss that is to miss everything. I think that's what James felt when he went on to say, "For what is your life? It is even a vapor that appears for a little time and then vanishes away" (4:14). The image is of the morning mists or fog that hovers around the peak of a mountain and then dissolves as the sun rises and the winds blow.

Life is like that. Our purpose is to know, love, and glorify the Lord and become prepared to live with Him forever. And in the brief span of this life He will guide our thinking and willing to accomplish His plan for us. I've never known a person to have a nervous breakdown doing what the Lord wills. He never asks us to do more than He is willing to provide strength for us to do. He does not guide us into a burnout. The Spirit of the Lord in us is an eternal flame, and the promise made by John the Baptist is true for us: Christ baptizes with fire!

Ten words fan the fire of His Spirit in us. James tells us we are to say, "If the Lord wills, . . . I will do this or that" (4:15). There's the antidote to burnout, the motto of a beautiful life. Saying those words each hour of every day, in each decision, and in ordering our total life will bring peace and excellence. Success is doing what the Lord wants us to do. He will liberate our wills to implement our total nervous system to carry out what He guides in our thought processes. He prepares us for decisions that are ahead of us. In consistent times of prayer with Him each day, He gets us ready to make guided choices. And when we come up against a decision about which we do not feel sure, it is crucial to put off any choice until we have given Him time to build in us the clarity we need.

We've talked a lot here about the Lord's power to guide our wills to keep us from overload and burnout. We need also to deal with the burnout that comes from missing opportunities He has arranged for us. People burn out from lack of challenges as much as in trying to do too much. The Lord delights to press us into tasks crucial to the forward movement of His strategy for us and the Kingdom goals where we live—in families, places of work, churches, and communities. The problem of some people is not burnout but never having a flame to worry about burning out. James deals with that in a decisive way: "To know what is right and not do it, for us that is sin."

There's a stress caused by a dull, unadventurous life. It comes from the stifling of the strength the Lord gives us. It's holding Him off, saying no, not to life's demands, but to Him. We burn out because we do not flame the fire with obedience. We become dull, bland, unexciting people. Here again, the crucial thing is to ask the Lord what He wants for us in life's relationships and responsibilities. Our willingness provides the dry kindling for the Lord to set us ablaze.

"*Deo volente*" was the watchword of the early church. As a matter of fact, in many periods of history, the saints would end their letters with "*D.V.*," which means, "If God wills." Many of them would then follow it with another Latin phrase, "*Carpe diem*"—"Seize the day."

I like that. When we say, "*Deo volente*," we can also say, "*Carpe diem*." We will not burn out. Our constant prayer will be, "Whatever the Lord wills, I want to do with delight." Then we can live with freedom and joy in each day knowing that He will guide and direct each step of the way.

CHAPTER SEVEN

RESIGNING FROM THE
KINGDOM OF THINGDOM

One day I used my hand calculator to add up all the hours I had spent worrying over money since I was a young man on my own until now. Then I projected what time I would continue to spend if the syndrome persisted until I was eighty. When the figure 20,000 appeared on the little screen of my calculator, I was astounded.

If I LIVE UNTIL I AM EIGHTY, I WILL HAVE SPENT twenty thousand hours worrying about money.

I pay my bills twice a month. It takes me about five hours to go through them all and write all the checks. Stress often mounts when I get nearer the bottom of the stack and wonder if I'll have enough left to pay all I owe. As I pay them I groan inside over the high cost of living and question my own or my wife's expenditures. When some company's computer has overcharged me or not recorded a previous payment, I feel like a victimized number rather than a person who seeks to be financially responsible. And when I talk over bills with my family I've been known to be less than saintly! In fact, my wife used to know which days I'd paid bills by the way I looked and acted when I came home. Though the Lord has always met our needs and been gracious to pull us out of difficulties in times of financial crisis, I tend to forget that and become anxious.

Tax time is another stressful time. It takes me several days to prepare the material for my tax consultant. The review of all the checks from the past year is like reading my own autobiography! Keeping careful records is a challenge and I'm always missing some crucial stub or notation that takes hours to find.

Because I am responsible for the budget of a large church and our expanding television ministry, I also experience concern over income and outgo in that area. I firmly believe that when the Lord gives us clear guidance to do something, He will provide what is needed, but since He does that through the gifts of people, sometimes the flow is not consistent. For example, many people complete their pledges for the work of the church at the end of the year. That makes for tenterhook trust during lead periods of the year. I've never had an unbalanced budget at the end of any of my thirty years of ministry, but I've had some stressful hours wondering. As for our church's television program, it is underwritten entirely by the gifts of viewers. Because many religious broadcasters use crisis tactics in raising money, people have been conditioned to give when there is a do-or-die appeal. That requires strong money appeals and constant planning to keep a program on the air. I am not comfortable with such methods and trust the Lord for financial support through my friends in the viewing audience, so I spend several hours each week praying about money to support this national television ministry. Again, the Lord always meets the need without a dime to spare.

The question then is, if God knows and has consistently worked in people's hearts to give the exact amount needed, why do I experience stress over money during the period between praying about the need and His magnificent answers? The Lord constantly leads me into adventures in which He can surprise me with His intervening grace. Then why should I be concerned?

One day I used my hand calculator to add up all the hours I had spent worrying over money since I was a young man on my own until now. Then I projected what time I would continue to spend if the syndrome persisted until I was eighty. When the figure 20,000 appeared on the little screen of my calculator, I was astounded. That led to a deep time of prayer about the stress that finances cause me. The spiritual exercise was particularly relevant because I sensed the same problem in thousands of people who write me confiding their needs. Perhaps the Lord wanted to do something in me that could be helpful to share with others. I continued to think and pray about the question for months.

What I discovered was a hidden scar in my psyche from the impressionable years of childhood. I was raised in Kenosha, Wisconsin, during the last days of the depression. The economic valley of depression from which the nation was just beginning to emerge still held this small Midwestern industrial city in financial distress. Though my proud Scots father never allowed his family to think of itself as poor, we were. The stress of earning enough to eat and care for the bare necessities was a pervading frustration, and the fear of not having sufficient resources was ingrained in me. At the same time, my parents exemplified the dignity of self-reliance and hard work.

As a young boy I would take my wagon early in the morning, walk several miles out of the town to a farm where I would buy sweet corn to sell door to door. I would bargain with the farmer for the lowest price per dozen and then resell the corn for five cents a dozen more. Little by little, I built up enough capital to assist the family and eventually to buy my own first suit. I can still feel a warm glow when I recall that accomplishment. The suit had a coat and two pairs of pants. No longer did I have to feel the insecurity of being dressed in "hand-me-downs" when I went to social functions at school.

From the time I was thirteen, I earned any extra money I could call my own. At seventeen I was completely on my own. Except for scholarships I was fortunate enough to win, I had to work for every dime I've ever had. Any money borrowed to continue my education was paid back with extra hours of work after classes. The amazing thing was I always had just what

I needed. All through the struggle to get through college, seminary, and postgraduate school, I experienced a combination of opportunities to work and the good health to invest long hours on the jobs in addition to my studies. But I worried a lot about money.

My wife, Mary Jane, and I were married while I was still in college. We scrimped and carefully watched every dime. Long before my training for the ministry warranted it, I was given opportunities to work in churches to support my education. Even through those difficult years of college and seminary, we always had enough to eat and pay our bills. When the opportunity came for me to attend New College, of the University of Edinburgh, Scotland, for postgraduate studies, I did not have the funds to underwrite the cost. But one day a teacher I had known in Kenosha called and asked to see me. When she arrived, she said that I had been on her heart and she felt the urgent need to see me and ask if there were some concern troubling me. She had no prior knowledge of my opportunity for further study and my inability to accept because of lack of funds.

During our conversation that day, she kept probing until she uncovered my dream and the impossibility of realizing it. When she learned of the need, she said that she had saved through the years in order to be able to help some student go on in his or her education. The amount she had saved was exactly what I needed to go to Scotland and complete the postgraduate course. She loaned it to me, and I paid back the no-interest note over ten years after I returned and began my ministry. Again, the Lord had stepped in to help me through an angel of His love. Still, the fear of not having adequate resources persisted.

As I began my adult life engrossed in an active church ministry, this deep personal concern about money made me conservative in expenditures and diligent in saving. It wasn't until I began this present study of stress that I realized that even though I was comfortable financially, I still was carrying stress baggage into my financial matters. It was then that I became determined to do something about it.

I have told this story about the stress I feel over money because it reveals the impact of our background on present worries even when there may be no apparent cause. Your background may be very different from mine, but whatever it is, it is probably contributing to your attitude about money today.

Few things cause more stress in individuals, marriages, and families than finances. Many couples tell me they argue more over money than over any other subject. One frequent reaction to such arguments is to overspend compulsively because of tension over it. Another reaction is frustration over the crippling guilt when spending money for anything except bare necessities. We live in a society where money and the things it can buy are a standard of our success, a sign of our personal worth, a basis of competitive comparisons with others, and a weapon of manipulative control. Ours is the wealthiest nation in the world, and still money continues to be a prime cause of inordinate stress.

The question is, when is enough too much? I am amazed at how my perception of what is enough has changed through the years. It has moved from subsistence, to adequacy, to abundance. I've never met a person who has said that he or she had too much money. And people with too little are worried about getting more, while people with too much are frightened about keeping what they have.

At the same time our preoccupation over money fills our thoughts with stress-producing anxiety. Whether we are buying groceries or buying a company, the concern over money is signaling "red alert" to our limbic system. The result of our stress is pumped into our bloodstream whether we are struggling to pay our household bills or balance the books of a corporation. We wrangle over budgets at home, at the office, at church, or in some community organization. Some people feel stress over not having adequate funds for a vacation, while others feel stress on a vacation as they think about the bills from the credit card companies that will be awaiting them when they get home.

Inflation also has its worry toll. As the value of the dollar diminishes and prices escalate, we are troubled over what little our earnings can buy and the minimized worth of our carefully gathered savings. Those who are fortunate enough to have stock leaf through the pages of the morning newspaper to check what they are worth before reading the headlines about what's happening in the world.

Added to this is the worry most people have about retiring. A friend of mine went to his doctor for a final checkup before retiring. He had been a faithful employee of a large corporation for years. Each month for years, the company had retained a modest amount for his retirement years, in addition to his having paid into Social Security for over thirty years. As the doctor started to take my friend's blood pressure, he asked, "How are you?" The man replied, "I'm getting ready to retire!" And at the moment he said the word "retire," his blood pressure jumped higher.

"A little worried about retiring, are you?" the doctor asked.

That began a long conversation about the man's frustration over all the years of working hard, saving, and still not being able to retire without financial worries. This was causing him immense stress. He would probably have to seek employment after retirement to keep up the style of living he and his wife had become accustomed to through the years. He would have to defer all that he had anticipated doing with his leisure time. He confessed to his friend and physician, and later to me, that he felt like a helpless victim of inflation that had rendered his savings totally inadequate. But inadequate for what? Had enough become too much?

Meanwhile, advertising continues to dominate our perception of what is enough. We are bombarded with urging to buy and then to borrow to buy more. What others have becomes the standard of what we ought to have. Envy rooted in the combative competition we talked about in a previous chapter rears its ugly head. What can we do about the stress caused by money and material things?

In this book we have put a great emphasis on the cerebral cortex as the center of the stress-producing systems of the body. Therefore, if worry over money and possessions is sending "red alert" signals which are keeping us inordinately agitated, we must examine our thinking. What would it be like to have a cortex completely controlled with Christ's Spirit, truth, and attitudes toward what we earn, save, spend, buy, and give away? Are there some basic irreducible maximums that can transform our thinking and become the grid to exclude either worry or fear?

These were questions I asked myself when I discovered how much stress money was causing me because of the false conditioning of my background. Like so many Christians today, I had committed my life, including all my possessions, to the Lord. I realized that all I had and am was a gift of grace. Yet the inner child of my past in this area had not been healed and enabled to grow to the fullness of the stature of Christ. I had preached hundreds of sermons on stewardship through the years and had been a consistent tither of my income. But something more was needed to break the stress cycle that began in my thinking and surged into my body before I could get control of it.

I often had read James's prophetic condemnation of the misuse of wealth in 5:1–6. The cutting words seemed unrelated to my problem. He talks about the rich who are corrupted, who misuse the poor, and who will be judged for not sharing their wealth. I dismissed the passage as one that did not speak to my condition. Then one day I restudied those words in the original Greek. Verse 3 gripped my attention: "Your gold and silver are corroded, and their corrosion will be a witness against you and will eat your flesh like fire. You have heaped up treasure in the last days."

That seemed like strong language, which I had felt was applicable only to the wealthy. Then two things hit me. One was that I probably spent more time in concerns over money than many wealthy people—certainly as much. The second thing was James's vivid mixture of metaphors. The corrosion of the silver and gold reminded me of their impermanence and the false value we put on them. Corrosion could be another word for worry over wealth or the lack of it. It does not satisfy our deep inner needs, however much we have.

And the result? "It will be a witness against you and will eat up your flesh like a fire." In other words, our distress over finances "burns us up."

What a colorful description of stress! Just as corrosion acts on silver and gold to dull and tarnish their luster, so, too, worry over money corrodes and tarnishes our lives.

Physically, this is what happens when we are in a constant state of unrest. As we noted very early in this book, the sympathetic adaptation system supplies an excessive amount of what are called catecholamines, chemicals activated under stress. They increase the level of blood cholesterol, decrease the ability to clear the blood of this cholesterol, and cause the clotting elements of the blood (platelets and fibrinogen) to settle on the walls of the arteries of our bodies. Then the heart works harder to circulate blood. Once the coronary arteries become clogged, the heart fails. So, if concerns over money and things and needs persist over a long period of time, they may very well contribute not only to heart disease, but to the numerous other stress-related illnesses.

As I reflected on all of this, I decided that money and material possessions are really congealed personality. They are so much a part of us that they become an extension of our personhood. Most of the time we think of ourselves and others in terms of what we have, how we dress, where we live, how much we have in the bank, and what we can acquire. Our image of our-

selves and others is inseparable from material possessions, social status, and position. But when we commit
our lives to Christ it is impossible to give Him our
souls without relinquishing control of what we have
and will have in the future. The fragmentation of our
spiritual and material life is what causes the stress. A
portion of our cerebral cortex acknowledges Him as
Lord while other portions continue with a "what's
mine is mine" distortion.

Here are some practical steps for the transformation
of our thinking so that Christ can control our responses and actions in regard to all phases of money,
our material wealth, and possessions.

1. Remain aware that all that we are and have belongs to the Lord. It is not ours, but a trust from Him
to be managed with His guidance and direction. The
Psalmist said, "The earth is the Lord's and the fullness
thereof, the world and all those who dwell therein"
(Ps. 24:1, RSV). When that thought becomes the liberating memory factor in the computer of the brain, it
replaces the false idea that we own anything. We are
stewards of the natural world, the endowments the
Lord gave us, the training He enabled, and the opportunities to work and earn He's provided. The knowledge we've acquired through study has come from
revelation of truth He gave to generations before us
whether they acknowledged Him as the source or not.
Our capacity to understand, the will to work, the ener-

gy to expend, and the results of our labors are not ours but His.

I had heard, studied, and thought these truths long before they became the essential basis of my mind's control of my reactions to money and material things. Long after I became a Christian, I still considered what I had and could earn as my gift to God. That arrogance had to be broken before the stress it was causing could be alleviated. I spent several years as a Christian leader, using what I thought were my gifts for God's glory, giving my money for His works, and expending my energy helping people honor Him. I was thankful for the grace and strength to be able to work and earn so that I could live responsibly and care for my family and others. All this time I was so near, and yet so far, from the radical mind-reorienting truth that I could not breathe a breath, think a thought, or exercise my endowed talents if it were not for His moment-by-moment blessing and provision. No wonder the stress of self-effort was "eating at my flesh like a fire."

2. Keep in mind that a radical commitment of all we are and have breaks the stress syndrome. I have used the word "radical" carefully. It means "to the roots." I believe a radical commitment is a total reorientation of all thought around the conviction that we are responsible to the Lord for how we use the gifts He has entrusted to us. When we surrender the control center of

our thinking, our attitudes toward money and material possessions change. We no longer belong to ourselves.

3. Ask for guidance on how to earn, save, and spend according to the Lord's plan. It is liberating to discover how involved He is willing to be in how we acquire and spend our money. We can appreciate why when we reflect on how affected we are by our decisions about where and how we work, as well as what we earn and how we spend it. Misguided decisions can result in frustration and stress. We can miss opportunities He has prepared for us and can spend our way into trouble. Often seemingly insignificant decisions lead to momentous difficulties.

Is the Lord concerned about our daily choices when it comes to money? Yes! If the majority of our worries come from it and diminish our effectiveness, we can be sure He is ready and willing to help us. The key to financial management is Christ's own instruction to seek first God's kingdom and righteousness, and all things we *need* will be added to us (Matt. 6:33).

That's more than just good advice. When we ask to receive the mind of Christ to control our thoughts, He does more than remind us of His admonition; He actually gives us the thoughts, discernment, and will to implement it. He lives out His own challenge within us. We don't do it for Him; He engenders the insight we need to respond. Our minds become the realm of the kingdom—His reign and rule. He becomes the initiator and instigator of what we are to do, buy, save, sell, and give away. It all belongs to Him anyway. We have every reason to assume He can and will help us manage our financial affairs. It's His responsibility. Ours is to be receptive and responsive. When we really believe that He can take charge and help us, the stress over money begins to subside. But that's not all!

4. Remember that an attitude of gratitude is expressed in giving with freedom and joy. The tangible, biblical sign of our commitment to allow the Lord to be our financial manager is expressed in tithing and giving. You may be surprised that I augmented tithing with giving. Isn't tithing giving? Not according to the Bible. The tithe, the first tenth of the harvest, was considered to be the Lord's. What was His already could be offered in gratitude, but giving began after the tithe was returned.

This insight from a careful study of Scripture is the secret of establishing in our thought processes the idea that all that we are and have is the Lord's. It was for me.

For years, I was proud of the fact that I tithed. I kept elaborate books to be sure one tenth of everything I earned was committed to His work. Then I worked with the nine-tenths as if it were my own. No wonder I was under stress from money matters!

As I prayed about a solution to this stress, I was led to a deeper understanding of giving. My ideas changed. I began to enjoy giving from the nine-tenths. Instead of wondering how much I could afford to give, my question became: how much do I really need? That forced me to think about my lifestyle in comparison to the poor, the hungry, and the spiritually disadvantaged.

Giving to the church program of mission and evangelism and to people in need became a constant reminder that anything I possessed was not my own. And the amazing thing was that the more I gave, the more the Lord provided me.

5. Ask the Lord to guide you into opportunities to share in which He provides the additional resources to follow through. Nothing has helped me and so many of my friends reorient our thinking about money than this.

The formula is to tithe, then give to the fullest of your ability, and then pray for opportunities to be shown you for which the Lord will entrust the above-and-beyond resources needed. For example, each year in our church on Mission Sunday we publish a long list of mission and evangelism projects. The people, most of whom are already tithing and giving from their income, ask the Lord for guidance as to which of the needs He wants them to be agents of blessing. Then we pray for the amount the Lord wants to supply us to give. And we yield our checkbooks to be a channel for the harvest of unexpected income and the writing of the check for the amount to be sent to the program or need.

We have been astonished by the way the Lord has answered, often in the exact amount of the faith promise. One man received a check in the mail which was a total surprise. The amount equaled the missions faith promise he'd made plus the amount of tax that would be due on the additional income! His own faith was quickened.

I could fill a whole book with stories like that. The crucial thing is what this has done to the financial stress level in the people who have participated in the adventuresome experiment. It has convinced them that the Lord is able, that He is involved in our financial needs, and that He can be depended on in the same way for personal financial problems. When we learn to trust the Lord to guide financial decisions, we discover His ability to enable financial provision.

I know it works. In these past few years I have been amazed at how consistent prayer gives wisdom in financial decisions in my own life and ministry. Often I am guided not to attempt things which would have been less than maximum for me. But at the same time, I am becoming bolder in attempting programs in the expansion of ministry than ever before. And on time, in time, the Lord supplies. The thing that broke the worry-stress syndrome for me was the repeated intervention the Lord accomplished in my own personal giving.

Now I want to correct the statement with which I began this chapter. I do not plan to have spent twenty thousand hours worrying about money by the time I'm eighty. What the Lord has done to invade my thoughts and control the signals to my body systems has changed that calculation. I made that discovery after I'd been a Christian for twenty-five years. Now I'm well into the second half of the adventure. Between now and eighty will be more than enough stressless hours to balance off my stress-filled hours before I resigned from the kingdom of thingdom. Regret over what I missed is offset by the excitement of the adventure ahead. The inner child of the past, conditioned to worry over money, has been given the privilege of growing up.

CHAPTER EIGHT

RACEHORSES

AND TURTLES

Impatience can become what I call the "worry fix." We become so accustomed to being agitated by the stress it produces that it actually becomes uncomfortably unfamiliar to be free of any distress. Like dope addicts, we need a fix to return us to the condition to which we've become accustomed.

DID YOU EVER WISH YOU COULD CHANGE THE people in your life? Do you ever become impatient with them? If you had a magic wand and could wave it over your loved ones or friends or people with whom you work and immediately change them, what would you change?

If you're like me, many people come to mind. Also, like me, you probably realize that you have a clear agenda for what you want them to be and do. I think I know exactly what is best for them, how they should change, and the kind of people they should be.

There used to be a popular television program called *Queen for a Day*. It awarded the winning contestant with a full day of activities and prosperity fit for a queen. I have a friend who likes to ask, "If you were king what would you do?" It's his way of helping people to consider what they'd do to solve problems and grasp opportunities if they had the power to decide. Another way of asking that is, "If you had absolute authority, what would you do?" In considering these questions suddenly we are aware of the frustrations we have been suppressing about people we wish we could change. It's amazing how much turmoil we have boiling inside of us about people we long to remake according to our specifications.

Impatience with people is a major cause of excessive stress in our lives. We all experience it, but it is the particular proclivity of a personality type I want to discuss in this chapter. Most of us who suffer inordinate stress belong to this category. If not, we are probably feeling stress from the pressure of those who are.

The late Hans Selye, recognized during his life as the preeminent investigator of stress, divided people into two categories. Some of us are what he calls racehorses who thrive on a fast-paced life, are highly motivated, competitive, aggressive, and often long for challenges, adventure, even danger. Others of us are turtles who move slowly, require peace and quiet, and are cautious and careful.

Racehorses tend to be very impatient with turtles. They find it difficult to get them to do what they want, when and how they want it. Their impatience is expressed in an attitude of frustration and judgment. They give the impression that there is something wrong with those who don't run at their pace, think as they do, and respond to their time schedule. Racehorses want everything yesterday. They are what is called type A personalities.

Modern medicine and psychiatry have divided people into three personality types, A, B, and C. In a book entitled *Type A Behavior and Your Heart** cardiologists Meyer Friedman and R. H. Roseman discuss the importance of personality patterns in stress and heart disease. Type A people are characterized by racehorse behavior: excessive impatience focused in insecurity, need for recognition and accomplishment, frequent dissatisfaction with life, a struggle with an overloaded schedule, and often a free-floating hostility. The cardiologists say that up to 50 percent of the United States population falls into this category. The difficulty with type A people is that they usually want everyone to march to their music, at their tempo and timing, and under their upbeat direction.

About 40 percent of people are type B. Like Selye's turtles, they are less demanding on themselves and others. They live at a slow pace and are able to adjust to the slow progress of others around them. Goals are less strenuous and performance less crucial. Because egoism is not the dominating attitude, they are more conciliatory than competitive.

The other 10 percent fall into category C, those who have a mixture of both A and B traits. With half the world made up of B and C types, the racehorses are

*New York: Fawcett, Crest Books, 1978.

constantly faced with the problem of impatience. They are perturbed by the slow progress of people, groups, companies, and institutions. There is an urgency to get on with life and they are frustrated when others do not share their demanding timetables. They are driven by the feeling that if they don't do something, it won't get done, or if it's done, it won't be done right. Type A people usually express immense impatience with type B people when they are trying to work together in a group. The same thing happens in marriage, between parents and children, among friends, and in our relationships at work or in the church.

I know—I've been a type A racehorse. Also, I suspect many of you who are reading this book are too. It may be the reason for your concern about the stress you're experiencing and the desire to discover how to cope with it. We know the stress that pulsates within us when we become impatient with other people. Our question is how to affirm the positive aspects of our type A personalities and use our energies more creatively without condemnatory judgments on other people, especially the turtles of our lives.

Recently a woman came to see me about the problem of mounting stress in her life. Her family physician recommended that she see me. He had identified stress in her life as the cause of her high blood pressure and many other related ailments. As she talked about herself and her life, her type A personality was expressed in her attitudes about people, especially her husband. "I love him," she said, "but his laid-back attitude about everything makes me want to scream! He thinks, talks, and acts so slowly. There's no drive, enthusiasm, or zest. I'd like to plant a bomb under his easygoing personality. When I can't seem to change him or our life together, I get frustrated and agitated." Her impatience had been turned in on herself. The explosion she wanted in her husband was really taking place in her own nervous system and was affecting her health.

The more we talked, the more I was aware of the problem of judgmentalism in this racehorse woman about her turtle husband. The implication was that *she* was right and something was wrong with her mate because he didn't react the way she did. She gave the impression that God really wanted everyone to be racehorses. Several visits and prayer together helped her to accept the fact that her impatience with her husband was not changing him and was making her ill. Though she had been an active Christian most of her life she had never committed her life and marriage to God. When she did that, the energies she was expending in trying to run the lives of her loved ones were turned into creative activities of growing in and sharing her faith. When she surrendered her husband to the Lord, new love for him surged within her. The stress produced by her impatience subsided and her physical symptoms disappeared.

James gives us the secret of how to overcome the

stress caused by impatience. In James 5:7–12 we are provided the key to developing an attitude of patience.

I am thankful that the New Testament spans the period of growth and expansion of the church to include converts who struggled with how to experience Christ's control of their thoughts and the transformation of their attitudes of impatience. James identified impatience as a perplexing problem among the racehorses of the early church. Note in this passage how he challenges them to be patient, and especially to be patient with one another. "Therefore be patient, brethren, until the coming of the Lord. See how the farmer waits for the precious fruit of the earth, waiting patiently for it until it receives the early and latter rain. You also be patient. Establish your hearts, for the coming of the Lord is at hand. Do not grumble against one another, brethren, lest you be condemned. Behold, the Judge is standing at the door!"

James's words offer three gifts to us racehorses to help us maximize our personality type in a really creative way, and at the same time overcome the impatience that cripples our relationships. We can live on the Lord's timing, our energies can be multiplied by the supernatural power, and we can accomplish a greater purpose than our compulsive goals. The Lord is not against racehorses. But He wants us to bring our personalities and the attitudes we express under His control and be employed for His plan, our ultimate productivity, and the building up of others.

Consider first what it means for a racehorse to live with the Lord's timing. James's assurance of the Lord being at hand implies his expectation of the Second Coming. Obviously, the Lord didn't return when James anticipated. People through Christian history have tried to predict when that blessed event would happen. It could be today or any day. But at the core of that anticipation is a confidence that puts into a new light the stress caused by our impatience with people and life itself. The Second Coming reminds us that history as we know it will eventually be brought to an end with the Lord's return. That sets us free of our tight grip on life and our worry over ourselves and other people's performance. The Lord is in charge. He controls not only when history will be culminated but everything that happens between now and then.

Racehorses can relax—we belong to the Lord; our capacity to run on the fast-track, the track of life itself is His; and our destination is to glorify Him and not ourselves. The only hope for the transformation of type A personalities is to surrender our lives, talents, and immense ambition to the Lord. We will be helpless victims of inordinate stress until we do. The word *surrender* catches our attention. It startles our "we-can-win-if-only-we-run-faster" tendencies.

That's what happened to Paul. He was a racehorse with religious zeal that was squandered on the wrong goals and purposes. Then when he was encountered on the road to Damascus, he was convinced that the very

Christ whom he persecuted was not only alive but was the Lord of all life. "What do you want me to do?" he asked, bringing all his fragmented capacities under the Lord's control. The Apostle kept on asking that question all through his life. The answers he received didn't slow up his pace; in reality they accelerated it. The great difference was that he ran in a new direction, doing what the Lord guided and on His timing.

The Apostle explained the radical transformation of his personality in Galatians 2:20. "I have been crucified with Christ; it is no longer I who live, but Christ lives in me; and the life which I now live in the flesh I live by faith in the Son of God, who loved me and gave Himself for me." The surrender of his life was a crucifixion of Paul's aggressive, compulsive, and ambitious racehorse personality. He died to his determined control of himself and others.

Christ raised up a new Paul. Now his personality type was conditioned by Christ's indwelling presence in the Apostle's mind, emotions, will, and body. His talents were maximized; he was given capabilities he never had before; and he lived in the flow of divine energy, wisdom, and love so much greater than he had had before, that he astonished himself and amazed the world. One of history's greatest racehorses was no longer riding off in all directions, dissipating his energies. He was running under control, on the Lord's track and with superhuman strength. The same can happen to us racehorses today.

We underline our central theme again. The secret of Paul's immense creativity was that he lived under the control of the "mind of Christ." He had experienced the power of the challenge he made to the Philippians. "Let this mind be in you which was also in Christ Jesus . . ." (Phil. 2:5). In Greek the "mind of Christ" may also be translated as the attitude of Christ, and we see that exemplified during His life on earth. Note this carefully, and with awe, for His attitude can become the controlling, guiding factor in us.

Christ lived in total dependence on the power of God flowing through Him. He knew where He had come from and where He was going. His purpose was clear. Jesus was not surprised by the perversity of human nature nor was He overcome by impatience with the bondage of will that kept people from being and doing what they were meant to be and do. Never in a hurry, He had time for prayer and for people. The Master lived on His own agenda and refused to be rushed, restrained, or manipulated by either His friends or His enemies.

It's comforting to remember that the disciples called to follow Him were mostly all type A racehorses—impatient people filled with the stress of their own agendas and desires for aggrandizement and eager for immediate changes. James and John, called Sons of Thunder, are good examples. They were energetic, take-charge men who were constantly at odds with the Lord's message and methods. Thomas, whose image has been blurred and blunted as "the doubter," was really a courageous disciple and always ready for a confrontation. Judas was also the personification of impatience. He had joined Jesus' disciples in hope that He would lead a military insurrection. I am convinced that his betrayal was an effort to force the Lord's hand and push Him into calling forth the legions of heaven to do battle with Rome.

Judas's suicide shows the ultimate impatience of not being able to control circumstances by human force. His anger was turned against himself. Peter also failed the Lord with his betrayal, but turned to the Lord in response to His forgiveness and the chance of a new beginning.

When Christ fulfilled His promise to abide in His disciples, a new breed of racehorses was released to live by His indwelling power and guidance. Type A personalities were harnessed, and they displayed the mind of Christ. His attitude was now in them. These early Christian leaders, and, a few years later, Paul, exemplify the patience that resulted. They loved people profoundly and trusted the Lord with the results. Living moment by moment with the conditioning of their attitudes by the mind of Christ, they overcame their racehorse impatience with the slowness and failures of others.

Listen to Peter: "And above all things have fervent love for one another, for 'love will cover a multitude of sins'" (1 Pet. 4:8); or to John, "In this is love, not that we loved God, but that He loved us and sent His Son to be the propitiation for our sins. Beloved, if God so loved us, we also ought to love one another" (1 John 4:10–11); and to Paul, "Let all bitterness, wrath, anger, clamor, and evil speaking be put away from you, with all malice. And be kind to one another, tenderhearted, forgiving one another, just as God in Christ also forgave you . . . and walk in love, as Christ also has loved us and given Himself for us . . ." (Eph. 4:31–32, 5:2). There's solid evidence of the transformation of the previously misdirected personalities of racehorses! Perhaps we could call them "double A" personalities, A types who superseded their category by the inspiration of the mind of Christ.

And you and I are meant to be among them. It can happen today. I know. Since Christ took charge of my life, my racehorse personality has been channeled into His purposes. And His indwelling love constantly frees me from judgmental impatience with others. I'm still a racehorse, but Christ's racehorse, seeking to be responsive to His reins to do what He wants by His enabling power and not my own.

This has made me sensitive to the needs of other racehorses. Over the years, it has been one of the great joys of life to care for them, be understanding of their personality proclivities, and eventually help them surrender their restless ambition and impatient natures to Christ.

With them, I continue to discover the second promise inherent in James's admonitions about patience. Not only is the Lord at hand, but He is able to take the concerns and frustrations that make us impatient and resolve them with His timely interventions. James gives us a simple but powerful parable about how to do that: "See how the farmer waits for the previous fruit of the earth, waiting patiently for it until it receives the early and latter rain" (5:7b).

Planting the seed is our commitment to the Lord of what causes us impatience. That's our task. We place it in the ground of faith. The people, what they do, and the circumstances that make us boil with the stress of impatience must be turned over to the Lord. Then He begins to work within the people and the situations frustrating us. That's the rain that softens the earth around the seed and nourishes it through germination and the first sprout of growth. "The early and latter rain" image reminds us that the Lord is constantly at work and does what we could not accomplish with our impatient criticism. The secret of turning stress into eustress, good stress, is in the complete commitment of our concerns. When we accept that we are not ultimately in control, we can stop trying to be in charge of people's lives and our program for their lives. The energies that would have been misused in fitful stress are used to affirm the people we have committed to the Lord in expectant faith.

I have a friend I've been worried about because of the way he has misused his immense talents and gifts.

He has jumped from one job to another without settling down, and he has failed to complete his education.

In our conversations I always expressed my concern and hope for him, affirming my belief in his potential. But one day I became aware of how my impatience was causing stress. Each time I thought of my friend, my pulse quickened, I became judgmental and angry, and felt agitated for hours afterward. That led me to pray more consistently about him.

As time passed, James's word about planting, watering, and waiting for the harvest thundered home to me that I had not planted a courageous seed of faith about this brilliant young man. I did that, claiming that the Lord, in His own timing and way, would break through to this young man about his future. Then I waited. Months went by. Whenever we visited, my temptation was to push or use guilt-producing tactics. By the Lord's grace I was able to withstand the urge.

After another long period of waiting, I received a phone call from him. Through circumstances I could never have arranged, the young man had been confronted with what he was doing with his life. Joy, not negative stress, surged within me when he told me about his decision to return to school and pursue his newly defined goals for his life. The Lord had used a person I would not have expected to enable the transition.

We all have people in our lives who cause us to be stressfully impatient. But instead we are to plant a courageous seed of trust—to know the Lord has a plan, and He will bring it to fruition. The same thing applies to the program and projects in which we are involved. Asking the Lord for a clarification of what He wants enables us to pray confidently and then wait. The bind of impatience cannot be broken without that.

There are three crucial words used by James in this section of his epistle that gives us a progression in developing the Lord's attitude toward people and organizations that cause us impatience. In Greek they are *hupomeno*, to remain under; *makrothumeo*, to be long-tempered; and *sterizo*, to establish, stabilize, or to make stable. The first two words are both translated as "patience" in English. However, they reveal two aspects of real patience.

To "remain under" means to accept the Lord's conditioning of our attitudes, to reshape them to be like His own. The most creative way of doing that is to form an image in our minds of how He would act, react, speak, and care in the same circumstances. Often it's helpful to picture the Lord in the actual situation or in response to particular people. The more we do that, the more our general attitude will be transformed.

That's important because stress reactions occur so quickly among the cortex, limbic system, and physiologic adaptation. Our impatience flows—in stress—

in our bloodstream long before we become aware of it. Consistent communion with Christ changes that. When we recognize the present causes of impatience, it prepares us for future attacks of this syndrome.

The second word for patience, *makrothumeō*, describes what happens as a result. The word is a compound of *makros*, "long," and *thumos*, "tempered." "Temper" is a word that describes the quality of attitudes, the characteristic frame of our minds. Another way of putting it is that attitudes are congealed thought and the expression of those attitudes comprises our temperament. We talk about quick-tempered or even-tempered people. But Christ makes us long-tempered. We are enabled by Him to wait for His perspective and power. So many of the things we regret in the expression of our impatience are caused by reacting before we've prayed for the mind of Christ.

How do we become long-tempered? I know of no other way than through the experience of the Lord's patience with us. A good exercise in becoming a patient person is to take a period of time for reflection with a pen and paper handy. List the times the Lord gave you a second chance, forgave you when you least deserved it, and did not turn away from you in spite of what you did to Him, yourself, and others. Then add to the list all the times that things over which you agonized worked out in a way you could never have planned or engineered on your own strength. As you reflect on that list, a time of gratitude for all His undeserved grace will set your heart singing and will condition your attitudes for future times when impatience with others strikes.

The third word describes the result of the experience of both words for patience. It is *sterizō*, which means to establish, make stable, strengthen, firmly fix on a foundation. James challenges us to establish our hearts—our intellect, emotion, and will. This is the point of contact with the Spirit of Christ and His dwelling place in us. To establish our hearts is to make them consistent with His nature, to build all thought, emotion, and decisions on His mind and attitude. Really, it is the Lord who establishes us.

That's what Paul meant when he used this same word at the conclusion of Romans in one of the "He is able" affirmations. "Now to Him who is able to establish you . . ." (Rom. 16:25). The secret of allowing Him to do that is in what Paul had challenged earlier in Romans, "I beseech you therefore, brethren, by the mercies of God, that you present your bodies a living sacrifice, holy, acceptable to God, which is your reasonable service. And do not be conformed to this world, but be transformed by the renewing of your mind, that you may prove what is that good and acceptable and perfect will of God" (Rom. 12:1–2).

The word "bodies" really means our lives. In the context of our thoughts about the stress of impatience, the meaning is to offer our minds and the things that hassle us as a sacrifice of thanksgiving. We don't really get free of the problems that cause impatience until we thank the Lord for what He will do through them and what we will learn from them. The ultimate stage of relinquishment of our distress is to praise the Lord for it. That may seem strange, but it works.

When we pray about the people and situations that have us in a bind of impatience and actually thank the Lord for what we are going through and what He will do to help us, we are mysteriously released to receive what He wants to provide to establish His attitude in us. As a result we will not be conformed to the world's ways of reacting, but will be transformed by His renewal of our minds. The word "transformed," as used here, means congruity between inner thought and outward expression. We will be able to communicate patience in the most creative way.

An example of how this works out in practical daily pressure was expressed by a woman who is a fellow adventurer with my wife and me in the quest of the Lord's management of stress. She is a person who has the explosive combination of deep concern for people and a short fuse over their behavior. Our friend is a racehorse, type A, fast-track individual. She thinks quickly, moves swiftly, and has high standards for herself and everyone else. Her experience of faith did not come through a traumatic experience of failure or brokenness, so she finds it difficult to empathize with people who struggle.

This friend and her husband are in a small group

that meets regularly for Bible study and prayer. At one of the meetings she confessed the stress she was living with because of her recurring impatience with almost everyone in her life. The group enabled her to talk it out without interruption or glib advice. At the end of her explanation, she said, "I really want to be different. Talking this out has made me realize how little of Christ's attitude controls either my reactions to people or the inner stress that results. I want the group to pray for me in the next weeks that I might begin to be more sensitive and understanding of the people in my life."

With that she began to cry. She had turned off most of the people in her life by her impatience and was feeling the loneliness of her "righteous" indignation. The group gathered around her and prayed for her.

In the weeks that followed, she kept a log of her feelings and reactions. At the beginning of each day, and in each encounter with people, she consciously yielded her attitudes for Christ's guidance. A few startling evidences of a change of attitude convinced her she was on the move and built up her confidence. She began praying through encounters and meetings that previously had tied her in knots. That relaxed her and opened her up to Christ's conditioning. And she was amazed by how peaceful she felt inside. Each time the group meets she reports on what's happened. She's on the way—still a racehorse in all she enjoys doing, but different in that the purpose of the race has changed and the prize is not trampling on turtles, but being to others the patient person Christ has been to her.

Impatience can become what I call the "worry fix." We become so accustomed to being agitated by the stress it produces, it actually becomes uncomfortably unfamiliar to be free of any distress. Like dope addicts, we need a fix to return us to the condition to which we've become accustomed. But what's really needed is a prolonged period free of the stress so that new memories of what it is like to live at a lower stress level can be produced. Our mind's memory bank must be reprogrammed.

There's hope for us racehorses! The Lord has great plans for us in the work of communicating His love and power to others. Our personalities can be transformed so that our attitudes reflect the indwelling mind of Christ.

That requires time and one of the most creative of all therapies—meditation. It is to this antidote, the newly rediscovered stress relaxant, that we turn our attention in the next chapter.

CHAPTER NINE

HOW TO
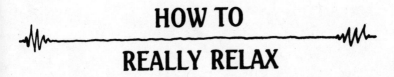
REALLY RELAX

*An unwillingness to meditate each day may be an ex-
pression of a lack of self-affirmation. Why else would we
deny ourselves the time to lower our stress level and become
prepared to live more abundantly?*

HARVARD CARDIOLOGIST HERBERT BENSON HAS discovered that teaching his patients meditation has brought measurable results in helping them cope with the inordinate stress of our times. He believes that meditation releases a built-in mechanism that causes such significant physiological changes as decreased heart rate, lower blood pressure, and amelioration of other stress-related symptoms.

This "relaxation response" through meditation is an alternative to the fight or flight emergency response which he deems inappropriate for today's social stresses. Utilizing the methods of Transcendental Meditation, he helps his patients discover how to meditate from ten to twenty minutes a day.

Dr. Benson's patients are taught to sit in a comfortable position, close their eyes, concentrate on a simple word, sound, or phrase, and exclude all other thought.

The significant difference from traditional TM is that patients are encouraged to select their own mantra, the word or phrase to be repeated in gaining thought control. Patients who have strong religious beliefs are free to select a word, phrase, or name sacred to their spiritual heritage.

Another form of relaxation through thought control being used by stress therapists today is biofeedback. By means of machines that monitor blood pressure, muscle tension, and body temperature, patients become aware of what's happening in their bodies. They learn how to relax, lower their blood pressure, release tight muscles, and lower body temperature. A person is first connected to the biofeedback machines by sensor detectors. After a number of sessions, during which a person learns the power of thought control on relaxation, he or she is taught to picture the same results through meditation. The idea behind this is that involuntary body responses can be brought under volitional control of our conscious mind.

We are living in what has been called the relaxation boom. And meditation with the help of special techniques or monitoring machines is being touted as a bonanza. This may force us to realize a secret we've known but not utilized—a quiet time each day can combat stress, change our attitudes, and transform our lives.

But we need to go much deeper in discovering what meditation really is. For a Christian it can be more than gaining control of bodily responses; it can bring our total being into contact with the Lord. Up to this point in our discussion of stress, I have illustrated how prayer actually helped people deal with stress. Now I want to examine a particular kind of prolonged prayer called meditation. All that Dr. Benson has discovered can happen through the use of Transcendental Meditation to elicit a built-in "relaxation response," can happen through a daily devotional time. And so much more!

At a crucial time in Jesus' ministry when He and His disciples were being besieged by the needs of people, He said, "Come aside by yourselves to a deserted place and rest a while" (Mark 6:30). The words actually mean, "Come away for yourselves and rest a while." The Lord wants us to love ourselves as loved by Him and give ourselves the gift of time each day for stress-reducing communion with Him. An unwillingness to meditate each day may be an expression of lack of self-affirmation. Why else would we deny ourselves the time to lower our stress level and become prepared to live more abundantly?

While becoming involved in my study of stress and what it was doing to me and others, eventually the new scientific emphasis on relaxation meditation made me take a look at my own personal daily time of prayer and Bible study. Ever since I became a Christian, I have had a quiet time each day. But in the past few years, I've tried to utilize that time as an antidote to stress.

I've shared the idea with others and they've joined me in a prolonged experiment. What we've discovered is very exciting.

The important thing that a daily time of meditation makes possible is the actual change of our mental attitudes as well as our bodily response. We place ourselves at the disposal of the healing Spirit of the Lord. James asks, "Is anyone suffering? Let him pray. Is anyone cheerful? Let him sing psalms" (James 5:13). Actually, creative meditation includes both prayer for our suffering and praise for the Lord's help in spite of everything. We can talk to Him about the difficulties and delights of life. He helps us overcome our hard times of suffering and truly enjoy our times of praise. And soon the praise over His interventions gives us a hopeful resiliency for the future. Here's how that can help in our lives.

The first step is to commit thirty minutes of each day to prayer meditation, fifteen minutes in the morning and fifteen minutes at the end of the day. That's a small part of the sixteen or more waking hours we all have. Many of my friends found it difficult to imagine taking an amount of time like that, especially for the rest of their lives. Consequently, some began a month's experiment, with the result that most of them have found it such a helpful experience that they have continued it. They are as enthusiastic about the stress-reducing power of prayer meditation as joggers are about exercise. Some have even added more time to the fifteen minutes, morning and night.

The purpose for both the morning and evening periods is the same—enabling oneness of mind, spirit, and body with the Lord—but since our needs are somewhat different at each of these times of day, I will explain them separately.

The important thing is to set aside the time and place as sacred, a meeting time with our Creator *and Recreator*. It should be set before or after breakfast and before the day's activities begin. Many have found it important to use the same place in their home. If you live in a family, explain why you are taking this time alone with the Lord. In addition to your Bible, get a good notebook for journaling a daily log of needs prayed for, what happened as a result, and an autobiography of your unfolding adventure of prayer. Writing down what happens to us will be a great source of encouragement in future times of need.

Once we are seated alone, we are ready to begin. I find it helpful to sit with my hands open, comfortably resting on my lap. That's a physical sign of our release of ourselves to the Lord and our willingness to receive what He has to give us. Closing my eyes, I focus on the Lord, who He is, what He has done for me through the cross, and what He has revealed He is able to do in receptive people. I repeat the names by which the Lord has been called describing His power, love, forgiveness, and intervening grace. Often I sing one of the great hymns I like, "Praise ye the Lord, the Almighty, the King of Creation," or a folk tune like "Father, I adore You, I place my life before You, How I love You!" Praise opens us up to the inflow of the Lord's Spirit. I like to visualize the infilling of His Spirit in the parts of my brain, nervous system, limbic system, blood, and muscles. As I do I feel a deep relaxation flood through me.

The next step is to confess anything of which we are conscious that may stand between us and the Lord—or between us and any other person. At this point I imagine putting that attitude, willful resistance, broken relationship, or uncreative action into my open hands. Then I lift them up into the air as a gesture of letting go of them and accepting the forgiveness I know is in His heart because of Calvary. I reaffirm the basic conviction that there was a cross in the heart of God before it was revealed on Calvary. And since the Lord is unlimited by time and space, the same gracious, forgiving love revealed then is consistently the same in the time of confession. In fact, we confess not in order to be forgiven, but because we know we are forgiven already. The stress of guilty memories can be healed on a daily basis.

That brings forth profound thanksgiving. In assurance of that forgiveness I find it helpful to repeat one of the several assurances of pardon. Sometimes it's liberating to say it out loud as a priest to yourself. "In the name of Jesus and by the power of the cross, you are forgiven. Go in peace!"

At this point, I find it important to read a passage from the Bible and reflect on its meaning in my life. I believe the Bible was not only divinely inspired but also is uniquely used by the Lord to speak to us. The objective Word brings guidance and conviction to our subjective concerns. The Psalms, the Sermon on the Mount, the Gospel of John, Philippians, Colossians, Ephesians, Romans, and then 1, 2, 3 John are good places to begin. In an appendix at the end of this book I have listed passages that are particularly helpful in the reduction of stress.

Now it's time in our devotional period to allow our meditation to be completely open to the Lord's invasion of our attitudes and temperament. Allow your mind to drift. The Lord will guide you to areas about which He has something to say. So often He goes much deeper than the problems and needs that seem paramount. Fixing our attention on Him totally, we can pray, "Lord, speak to me, I'm listening. Use the processes of my thought to say what I need to hear, understand, do. I yield my thinking brain to You. Take from it untruth and misconceptions and place in it the guidance and attitudes which will be the creative memory factors to trigger the healthy functioning of my total body systems in keeping with Your will for me and others. Heal whatever is in me that responds with inordinate fear and anxiety to the stress-producing circumstances and relationships in which I live."

Then as we remain quiet and totally open, our thoughts are led to memories that need healing, problems we're facing that need the Lord's wisdom, and people who alarm or frustrate us. Now, thoughts form that we know come from beyond our own knowledge or understanding. We begin to see things differently with supernatural vision.

This shouldn't surprise us. The Lord created us to be receivers and transmitters of His mind. According to Psalm 8, He made us a little lower than the angels. The word "angels" here in the Hebrew is *Elohim*, God. The meaning is that God has made us a little lower than Himself! The psalmist goes on to explain why. Speaking of mankind, he says boldly, "You have crowned him with glory and honor. You have made him to have dominion over the work of Your hands" (Ps. 8:5b–6a).

No wonder God wants to get through to us! He has made us viceroys over the creation that belongs to Him. Our dominion, expressed in the management of our lives, is very strategic in His plans for us and the people around us. He needs our attention to brief us on what is His best for our lives, and He is more concerned with our stress level than we are! Anything that will render us incapable of experiencing our full capacities in living out His plan for our lives is His concern and He wants to heal it and set us free to live abundantly.

After a time of thought reorientation and attitude-conditioning reflection, we are ready to close our meditation time with intercession, supplication, and dedication. The time of allowing the Lord to invade our minds and heal our bodies has given us the insight data to know how to pray for others and ourselves. Now it is a great joy to be able to ask God for what He has told us He is ready to give. We can be specific, following the direction He has revealed. That makes for bold praying and freedom from worry over what we've prayed. The closing step of morning meditation is to dedicate the day and all that will happen to Him, thanking the Lord *in advance* for all we will experience of His grace and intervention in the ups and downs of the day ahead.

That kind of morning meditation starts the day off with a burst of anticipation and excitement. We will also feel a marked lowering of our stress level and a readiness to filter out what may cause distress throughout the day. Starting a day with that quality of communion heightens our awareness of the Lord's presence all through the day and reminds us of His availability to control our thought reaction. We will find we pray all through the day.

Even so, the kind of world in which we live, populated by the stress-producing people we all encounter, will bring us to the end of the day needing a further time of meditation. Now our major interest is to get perspective on the day so that when we go to bed we can sleep relaxed and receptive to remedial rest. Just as we get undressed for bed, so too we need to undress our minds. That's done by praising the Lord for the day we've spent. Ask Him to teach you anything you need to learn from the day's mistakes or difficulties. Seek His forgiveness for anything you said or did that denied Him, hurt others, or was less than He guided. Allow the warmth of that grace to enable you to forgive people who have caused you stress during the day.

Last, forgive yourself. I find that hardest of all. But I've learned that unless I do, I will toss and turn restlessly throughout the night. A surrender of our failures and an acceptance of the Lord's forgiveness makes all the difference. The Lord divided our lives into days and nights and ordained the night for sleep, not self-condemnation that keeps us awake.

After we have praised God for the blessings of the day and accepted and given forgiveness for its shortcomings, we are able prayerfully to do some relaxation exercises. First, breathe out and say, "Lord, I give You my feelings of stress." Next, breathe in deeply and say, "I receive Your healing power." Then commit each part of your body to rest, moving up from your feet to your head and brain. Allow each part to go limp, as if being held without your volition. And with that you are ready to rest in the everlasting arms of a loving Lord.

I have taken time and space here to share this daily plan of meditation because it has worked for me and many others. But, of course, this isn't the only way to establish and maintain vital contact with God's healing and energizing Spirit. Each of us must find a plan that works for us. The main thing is to open ourselves to the saturation of His love and wisdom.

The point is that relaxation is a result of something else. For us to tell ourselves or anyone else, "Just relax!" is foolish. That's why the current relaxation boom won't last. Real relaxation is the result of the assurance that we are loved and cherished and that nothing can happen that will ultimately hurt us. Only God can give that assurance. All He asks is that we exercise our free wills to report in to Him daily in a time of quiet meditation in which we give Him our full attention.

CHAPTER TEN

DON'T TAKE IT
ALONE

My only question was why I had waited so long to talk out my deep feelings with someone. I had fallen into the trap of thinking that after all the sermons I'd preached on confident faith and the books I'd written about victorious living, I had to exemplify strength and courage. But in so doing I'd closed myself off from one of the greatest sources of power: the healing power of fellowship, the remedial love and healing gifts entrusted to others.

OUR BATTLE WITH STRESS IS A LONELY ONE. WE tend to think we are the only people who suffer from the kind of distress we feel. At the same time, we fall into the trap of thinking that it is weakness to admit to having stress. We think we should be able to handle it without other people's help. This is particularly true of Christians who claim to have a vital faith: we get under a lot of stress, develop symptoms of stress-related disease, and feel we have not trusted God enough or prayed consistently enough. Perhaps we have not, but countless others share such feelings and in times when we feel an acute need for spiritual power, the Lord often chooses to mediate His grace to us through another sufferer, a "wounded healer" who knows what we are going through and can stand with us. A trouble shared is a trouble cut in half.

All too often our problem is seemstress. Don't get

out your pen to correct the copy. The typesetter didn't make a mistake. He didn't put an extra *e* in the place of an *a;* that's the way I wrote it. Every writer has the prerogative to coin a word now and then. So, mine is seemstress—the stress of trying to appear as if we "have it all together." This adds stress to the already mounting burden of stress within us. Even though we may be "coming apart at the seams," we make every effort to "seem" to be coping. And our greatest fear is that the stress under which we've been living, that has attacked our physical health, will crop out in some undeniable stress-induced sickness that we can't hide and all the world will know about the turbulence that has been brewing in us all along.

One of the elders of my church wrestled with this problem. She was suffering immense pain from arthritis. She had prayed and hadn't been healed, so she began to question herself, "How can I be a leader of others if I can't pray for myself and get results?" This was particularly troublesome to her in her responsibilities as an elder to pray for people during the final portion of our Sunday morning services and in special healing services. Feeling immobilized with self-incrimination, she talked out her concerns with me. My response was to assure her that her suffering put her in touch with the needs and feelings of others in a way that would enrich her prayers for them.

Continuing to minister to others has helped her endure her own pain. If we wait to be perfect before we allow the Lord to use us in ministry to others, we will never begin. The willingness to admit our own need honestly and confess that we are seeking the Lord's help and healing opens us up to the encouragement and strength the Lord wants to give us. And often, when we get involved in caring for others, our own stress is measurably reduced.

A pastor friend of mine discovered this in a very striking way. He has helped thousands of people through his vital communication of faith and his sensitive counseling skills. But somehow he had not realized how much the congregation he serves loved him. Then one day an old problem with ulcers recurred, and without knowing it he bled internally for some time. In a phone conversation with a friend he had said he wasn't feeling well and that the old problem with his ulcer seemed to be back in full force. As the afternoon wore on, she couldn't shake a pervading concern for him, so when her husband came home they went to check on him. They found him collapsed on his living room floor. He was rushed to the hospital where emergency treatment was administered and his medical condition was stabilized.

When my wife and I arrived at the hospital later that evening, we found the corridor filled with concerned, praying people. Then and in the days that followed there was a great outpouring of love which contributed in large measure to his speedy recovery. When I visited him in his hospital room, the walls were papered with cards of love and flowers filled the room to overflowing. The exposure of his need gave all the people whom he had helped an opportunity to express their love for him.

I have known the same healing power of love from people in my own life. When my wife was ill with cancer, for a long time I refused to talk about it. The stress built up. I felt I had to be strong for my wife, children, and friends who were distressed by Mary Jane's illness.

Then one day the members of a fellowship group with whom I meet regularly lanced the stress boil in my being and drained out the distress by forcing me to talk about it. They kept pressing me with further questions, tenderly expressed with sensitive love. I sobbed as I talked about my feelings, fears, and the anxiety for the future. The group prayed for Mary Jane's healing of cancer and the healing of the stress it was causing in me. After that therapeutic time, I felt a deep inner peace. My only question was why I had waited so long to talk out my deep feelings with someone. I had fallen into the trap of thinking that after all the sermons I'd preached on confident faith, and the books I'd written about victorious living, I had to exemplify strength and courage. But in so doing I'd closed myself off from one of the greatest sources of power: the healing power of fellowship, the remedial love and healing gifts entrusted to others.

That was the greatest denial of all. The honesty and

openness about our needs which I had taught so passionately through the years was being contradicted by my desire to be a paragon of Christian courage. Spiritual pride almost kept me from receiving what the Lord was waiting to give me.

The Lord is constantly seeking to bring us to Himself and others. He wants to break down the barriers in both the vertical and horizontal dimensions. Often He withholds the healing blessing we need for our stress until He can drive us into the loving arms of friends whom He wants to use as channels of His grace.

The concluding portion of James's epistle, 5:14–20, is a powerful reminder that we don't have to take it alone. He says, "Confess your trespasses to one another, and pray for one another, that you may be healed. The effective, fervent prayer of a righteous man avails much" (v. 16). Then he concludes by asserting that helping another person with his or her problems "will save a soul from death and cover a multitude of sins" (v. 20). He uses the strong language of helping people who wander from the truth. When we are available to help we not only help that person, but our own sins are covered. Now, what does this mean for us as we attempt to cope with stress?

It means a great deal, I believe, especially when we remember our previous explanation of sin—*hamartia*, or missing the mark. Anything that keeps us from the Lord is missing the mark. We are meant to experience His grace in our physical and spiritual needs, and a mutual, supportive caring for one another. We have talked a great deal about how the Lord heals our stress by conditioning and controlling the thought patterns in our mind. When we try to handle stress on our own without His help, we not only continue in the stress cycle, but also deny the help others can be as agents of His grace.

It is important to remember that stress is not a sin; it is a psychosomatic syndrome which may be incited by our refusal to allow the Lord to take charge of our thinking, attitudes, and temperament. That deeper independence is the sin. Therefore, I think it is proper to reword James's admonition to include any stress problem we face that needs to be shared with others so the Lord can release His power for us through them. "Confess your stress to one another, and pray for one another, that you may be healed. The effective, fervent prayer of fellow believers avails much. If anyone among you is suffering from stress because of confused thinking upsetting the nervous or body systems, and you help him, you will enable him to live a fuller and longer life, and in the process, your own stress management will be increased." That's not an effort to rewrite Scripture; it is simply a way of showing how the impact of James's original words apply to the particular maladies of stress, as we experience them today.

The Lord did not create us to be solo flyers. We were made with a built-in need for intimacy with Him and other people. When we allow others to know us and share our battle with stress, the relaxation response we talked about in the previous chapter is activated. Our stress level, including the symptoms it produces—blood pressure changes, an inordinate flow of catecholamines, and other physical problems—is reduced.

In addition to a consistent practice of meditation we need a few trusted friends with whom we can talk about the stress we are feeling. If we bottle up what's troubling us, we'll eventually blow off the lid, or stew in the juices of our own body stress chemicals.

These friends should be the kind of people we can trust implicitly—people who are open about their own needs. When we are under pressure of stress we don't need a Pharisee who will interrupt our catharsis with a long list of "oughts." Choose vulnerable people who are also grappling with stress and can punctuate our sharing with little more than a sensitive, "I understand, I've been through it too." Then when we've emptied the pressure cooker of steam, the person can ask questions and probe deeper to expose the attitudes that may be triggering our stress reaction.

As we share, several things need to be remembered that will free us to be honest and direct. It is possible that our perception of what's happening to or around us may not be rational or even right. The point is, that's how we feel, but there's little chance of getting clarity or changing until we talk out what we are feeling. It is well to remember, too, that usually it's impossible to talk out our feelings at first with the people who are directly involved. We need another person who has no axe to grind, one who will honor our feelings and give us the stress-reducing right to express them. Then we can go to the people who are directly causing the distress.

We all need a half-dozen people who are stress-sharing partners. And it is most helpful if these people face some of the same circumstances you do. For example, executives under stress find that talking to other leaders at their level is most creative. They have a mutual understanding of the pressures and can get to the point quickly and speak in shorthand directness. The same is true of women in industry—they have an immediate empathy for the problems women face in their evolving role in leadership positions. Housewives can be sensitive with other women grappling with their mutual problems of a husband's schedule, family pressures, and immense responsibilities of being a lover, manager, homemaker, chauffeur, recreational director, counselor, problem solver, referee of conflicts, and entertainer. The same is true for clergy, educators, social workers, doctors, and lawyers, etc. And it is equally true for people facing the challenges and problems of being single.

The main thing is to find people from whom you feel an accepting, nonjudgmental, encouraging attitude—people who would not be shocked by anything you have to talk out; nondefensive people who can express love in a way that enables a free reflection and demonstrates a willingness to help us solve the problems causing our stress. The most destructive stress is that which comes from feeling that there is no solution, no action to be taken, no hope left. Stress is greatly reduced by using the pent up energy to wrestle with the problem, talk about possible solutions, consider steps of action, and come to some conclusion about what our attitude should be as well as the direction to be taken.

Another creative source of help is a small group. When people come together to share their needs, study the Bible, and pray for one another, stress is greatly reduced. Many groups are being formed with the specific purpose of understanding the causes and cures of stress, and of being a help to each other. Sharing partners often are in the same group.

I know of several of these groups that have worked through the understanding of stress I've tried to communicate here in this book. They have a mutual understanding of stress and can readily diagnose in each other the deeper causes of times of distress. Each person is given a time to talk about the impact of life on his or her stress reactions. Others in the group then can share how they are working with a similar problem or have dealt with similar pressures. Members of the group then pray for each other, and they make themselves available for supportive conversations and phone calls between meetings. The result is that the participants no longer feel they must take the debilitating effects of stress alone.

One of these groups drafted a covenant of commitment to clarify its individual and united efforts to manage stress. It sounds a little like the twelve steps of Alcoholics Anonymous, but in this case, it is the group's effort to clarify in writing the basic convictions about what its members could do to deal with stress in their lives. They called it *Ten Things I Will Do to Realize the Lord's Healing of Stress*.

1. I recognize that stress is a major problem in my life.
2. I praise the Lord for the magnificent stress-coping mechanism He has given me.
3. I acknowledge the linkage between my thinking and attitudes and my body's stress-producing systems.
4. I am thankful that my body can produce eu-stress to assist me in meeting life's demands, challenges and opportunities.
5. I seek to yield my thinking brain to the conditioning and control of the indwelling Christ.
6. I will set aside a time each day for meditation so that Christ can guide my thoughts and attitudes, decisions and actions, relationships and responsibilities.
7. I will quickly admit my inadequacy to manage stress and will talk to trusted confidants, fellow

stress-strugglers, to release the build-up of stress, and receive from them encouragement and prayer.

8. I will meet consistently with my small group and seek to be as honest as I can be about how stress is affecting my life and what my attitudes may be doing to cause it.

9. I will pray daily for other members of the group claiming Christ's healing power for them.

10. I will be sensitive to the things I do and say that cause stress in the people of my life and will, whenever possible, work to bring changes in the institutions, organizations, and groups of which I am a part to diffuse the stress-inducing society in America today.

These steps apply to all of us. They also may be the basis for getting a small group of people together to help each other with stress. The way to start is to pray for guidance for six to eight people (never more than twelve) to meet with you. If you are really open to the Lord's provision, He will provide the people.

In addition to participating in a small group, we can become stress-healers in our relationships in the family and at work in diffusing stress. We all need an opportunity to talk out our thoughts and feelings and not be put on the defensive or have blame cast upon us. And that raises the question, Am I the kind of person to whom others can talk out the pressures and strains they are feeling? I want to be, but am I really?

My wife and I now schedule regular weekly times just to talk about our life together—our hopes and dreams, frustrations and stresses, as well as things we may be doing to cause stress in each other. An intense, overloaded schedule has made that necessary. It was a time of growth and freedom when I first allowed my wife to go through a whole year's schedule and circle the times we would have just for talking. The same thing is needed among friends to develop deep, caring relationships.

We need that at work also. People need to feel that they are not helpless victims of the system. When they are freed of the fear of losing their jobs because they talk out what they are thinking about their work and how they can become involved in improving the production or ambience around them, they become involved partners in progress. Then they are much more ready to help a superior and cooperate in lowering his or her stress level. Often the stress-management groups I talked about above are formed among Christians who work together in factories or offices. They not only help each other personally, but work together to alleviate stress.

Now, here is a final summary word about the kind of person who is able to turn distress into eustress. James says that "the prayer of a righteous man avails much." A righteous person is one who has been made right with God by faith in His love and forgiveness through Christ. That rightness starts with a surrender of his or her life to the Lord. In response the living Christ takes up residence in us.

The process of regeneration begins to make us like Christ. A new creation begins, transforming our total nature into the person we were created to be. He works to bring all aspects of the cerebral cortex, limbic system, and the autonomic nervous system back into perfect unity and function to produce just the right amount of hormonal balance to meet the demands of life. Our prayers "avail much" because they are open to the receiving of the mind of Christ as guide and control of what triggers our creative stress-producing mechanism.

The result is neither fight, flight, frustration, nor purposeless flow. Because we are relaxed by our security in the status of being the Lord's chosen and cherished people, and because we know that we will be given the strength and ability we need, we can become involved in helping others.

Since we have fought and won the battle with stress, we know how to pray, what to ask for others, and what to confidently expect in response from the Lord. Instead of being a stress-producing part of the problem, we will become part of the stress-healing ministry of the Lord.

If stress is the epidemic problem medical science has singled it out to be, and I think our study affirms that we have a challenge big enough to last us the rest of our lives. Deep love and caring for the people around us and our society as a whole calls us to continue our own discovery of Christ-centered stress control. What happens to us will give us the courage to pray for the same thing to happen through us to fellow strugglers. That's exciting to contemplate and accept.

All of the ten antidotes to stress in James's prescription which we've discussed in each of the ten chapters of this book, work. We can manage stress—with the Lord's help. He has given us a stress management system. All we have to do is ask Him to take charge of our mind, infuse our nervous system with His Spirit, and control our body's responses.

Here is a prayer that helps me when the stress of life threatens to engulf me. You may want to pray it for yourself . . . and others. It summarizes all I've tried to say.

Lord, I need Your help. I am feeling the strain of stress. My body is agitated by worry and fear. I confess to You my inability to handle it alone. I surrender my mind to You. Take charge of the control center of my brain. Think Your thoughts through me and send into my nervous system the pure signals of Your peace, power, and patience. I don't want to have a divided mind fragmented from Your control.

Forgive my angers rooted in petulant self-will. Make me a channel, a riverbed, of Your love to others suffering as much stress as I. Help me act on the inspiration You give me rather than stifling Your guidance.

Take charge of my tongue so that it becomes an instrument of healing. Make me a communicator of love and forgiveness as I cheer others on to their best.

I commit my schedule to You, Lord: help me to know and do Your will. Guide me in doing Your will on Your timing so that I don't burn out doing the things I don't really want to do, or fearing to do what is Your best for me. Set me free from the tyranny of acquisitiveness and the lust of seeking my security in things rather than in my relationship with You.

I long to be the person You created me to be and not anyone else. Forgive me when I take my signals of success from others and not You.

Most of all, Lord, help me to catch the drumbeat of Your guidance and live by Your timing. Here is my life—invade it, fill it, transform it. And I thank You in advance for the healing of my life and for giving me strength to conquer stress. Amen.

BIBLICAL ASSURANCES
FOR TIMES OF STRESS

The Assurance of the Lord's Presence

Deuteronomy 31:6: "Be strong and of good courage, do not fear nor be afraid of them; for the Lord your God, He is the One who goes with you. He will not leave you nor forsake you."

Psalm 9:9–10: "The Lord also will be a refuge for the oppressed, a refuge in times of trouble. And those who know Your name will put their trust in You; for You, Lord, have not forsaken those who seek You."

Isaiah 41:10: "Fear not, for I am with you; / Be not dismayed, for I am your God. / I will strengthen you, / Yes, I will help you, / I will uphold you with My righteous right hand."

Isaiah 43:2: "When you pass through the waters, I will be with you; / And through the rivers, they shall not overflow you. / When you walk through the fire, you shall not be burned, / Nor shall the flame scorch you."

Matthew 28:20: ". . . Lo, I am with you always, even to the end of the age."

John 14:18–21: "I will not leave you orphans; I will come to you. A little while longer and the world will see Me no more, but you will see Me. Because I live, you will live also. At that day you will know that I am in My Father, and you in Me, and I in you. He who has My commandments and keeps them, it is he who loves Me. And he who loves Me will be loved by My Father, and I will love him and manifest Myself to him."

Romans 8:38–39: "For I am persuaded that neither death nor life, nor angels nor principalities nor powers, nor things present nor things to come, nor height nor depth, nor any other created thing, shall be able to separate us from the love of God which is in Christ Jesus our Lord."

Hebrews 13:5: ". . . For He Himself has said, 'I will never leave you nor forsake you.' "

The Assurance of the Lord's Love

Zephaniah 3:17: "The Lord your God in your midst, / The Mighty One, will save; / He will rejoice over you with gladness, / He will quiet you in His love, / He will rejoice over you with singing."

John 14:21: "He who has My commandments and keeps them, it is he who loves Me. And he who loves Me will be loved by My Father, and I will love him and manifest Myself to him."

Romans 8:28: "And we know that all things work together for good to those who love God, to those who are called according to His purpose."

1 Corinthians 2:9: "But as it is written: / 'Eye has not seen, nor ear heard, / Nor have entered into the heart of man / The things which God has prepared for those who love Him.' "

1 John 4:10, 16, 19: "In this is love, not that we loved God, but that He loved us and sent His Son to be the propitiation for our sins. . . . And we have known and believed the love that God has for us. God is love, and he who abides in love abides in God, and God in him. . . . We love Him because He first loved us."

The Assurance of the Lord's Power

Isaiah 40:29–31: "He gives power to the weak, / And to those who have no might He increases strength. / Even the youths shall faint and be weary, / And the young men shall utterly fall, / But those who wait on the Lord / Shall renew their strength; / They shall mount up with wings like eagles, / They shall run and not be weary, / They shall walk and not faint."

Zechariah 4:6: ". . . / Not by might nor by power, but by My Spirit," / Says the Lord of hosts."

John 14:12: "Most assuredly, I say to you, he who believes in Me, the works that I do he will do also; and greater works than these he will do, because I go to My Father."

Acts 1:8: "But you shall receive power when the Holy Spirit has come upon you; and you shall be witness to Me in Jerusalem, and in all Judea and Samaria, and to the end of the earth."

Ephesians 3:14–21: "For this reason I bow my knees to the Father of our Lord Jesus Christ, from whom the whole family in heaven and earth is named, that He would grant you, according to the riches of His glory, to be strengthened with might through His Spirit in the inner man, that Christ may dwell in your hearts through faith; that you, being rooted and grounded in love, may be able to comprehend with all the saints what is the width and length and depth and height—to know the love of Christ which passes knowledge; that you may be filled with all the fullness of God. Now to Him who is able to do exceedingly abundantly above all that we ask or think, according to the power that works in us, to Him be glory in the church by Christ Jesus throughout all ages, world without end. Amen."

Ephesians 6:13–17: "Therefore take up the whole armor of

God, that you may be able to withstand in the evil day, and having done all, to stand. Stand therefore, having girded your waist with truth, having put on the breastplate of righteousness, and having shod your feet with the preparation of the gospel of peace; above all, taking the shield of faith with which you will be able to quench all the fiery darts of the wicked one. And take the helmet of salvation, and the sword of the Spirit, which is the word of God."

The Assurance of the Lord's Forgiveness

Psalm 103:9–12: "He will not always strive with us, / Nor will He keep His anger forever. / He has not dealt with us according to our sins, / Nor punished us according to our iniquities. / For as the heavens are high above the earth, / So great is His mercy toward those who fear Him; / As far as the east is from the west, / So far has He removed our transgressions from us."

Isaiah 44:22: "I have blotted out, like a thick cloud, your transgressions, / And like a cloud, your sins. / Return to Me, for I have redeemed you."

Isaiah 55:7: "Let the wicked forsake his way, / And the unrighteous man his thoughts; / Let him return to the Lord, / And He will have mercy on him; / And to our God, / For He will abundantly pardon."

John 8:11: ". . . Jesus said . . . , 'Neither do I condemn you; go and sin no more.'"

Romans 6:14, 8:1: "For sin shall not have dominion over you, for you are not under law but under grace. . . . There is therefore now no condemnation to those who are in Christ Jesus, who do not walk according to the flesh, but according to the Spirit."

2 Corinthians 5:17: "Therefore, if anyone is in Christ, he is a new creation; old things have passed away; behold, all things have become new."

1 John 1:9, 3:17–18, 20: "If we confess our sins, He is faithful and just to forgive us our sins and to cleanse us from all unrighteousness. . . . But whoever has this world's goods, and sees his brother in need, and shuts up his heart from him, how does the love of God abide in him? My little children, let us not love in word or in tongue, but in deed and in truth. . . . For if our heart condemns us, God is greater than our heart, and knows all things."

The Assurance of the Lord's Caring in Frustration

Psalm 55:22: "Cast your burden on the Lord, / And He shall sustain you; / He shall never permit the righteous to be moved."

Romans 8:16–18: "The Spirit Himself bears witness with our spirit that we are children of God, and if children, then heirs— heirs of God and joint heirs with Christ, if indeed we suffer with Him, that we may also be glorified together. For I consider that the sufferings of this present time are not worthy to be compared with the glory which shall be revealed in us."

Philippians 1:6: "Being confident of this very thing, that He who has begun a good work in you will complete it until the day of Jesus Christ."

1 Thessalonians 5:16–19: "Rejoice always, pray without ceasing, in everything give thanks; for this is the will of God in Christ Jesus for you. Do not quench the Spirit."

1 Peter 4:12–13: "Beloved, do not think it strange concerning the fiery trial which is to try you, as though some strange thing happened to you; but rejoice to the extent that you partake of Christ's sufferings, that when His glory is revealed, you may also be glad with exceeding joy."

The Assurance of the Lord's Thought Control

Psalm 139:17: "How precious also are Your thoughts to me, O God! / How great is the sum of them!"

Proverbs 3:5–6: "Trust in the Lord with all your heart, / And lean not on your own understanding; / In all your ways acknowledge Him, / And He shall direct your paths."

Isaiah 26:3: "You will keep him in perfect peace, / Whose mind is stayed on You, / Because he trusts in You."

1 Corinthians 14:33: "For God is not the author of confusion but of peace, as in all the churches of the saints."

Ephesians 2:5: "Even when we were dead in trespasses, [God] made us alive together with Christ (by grace you have been saved)."

Colossians 1:27: "To them God willed to make known what are the riches of the glory of this mystery among the Gentiles: which is Christ in you, the hope of glory."

1 Timothy 1:17: "Now to the King eternal, immortal, invisible, to God who alone is wise, be honor and glory forever and ever. Amen."

1 John 5:14–15: "Now this is the confidence that we have in Him, that if we ask anything according to His will, He hears us. And if we know that He hears us, whatever we ask, we know that we have the petitions that we have asked of Him."

The Assurance of the Lord's Help in Anxiety

John 14:27: "Peace I leave with you, My peace I give to you; not as the world gives do I give to you. Let not your heart be troubled, neither let it be afraid."

Romans 15:13: "Now may the God of hope fill you with all joy and peace in believing, that you may abound in hope by the power of the Holy Spirit."

Ephesians 2:13–14: "But now in Christ Jesus you who once were far off have been made near by the blood of Christ. For He Himself is our peace, who has made both one, and has broken down the middle wall of division between us."

Philippians 4:6–7, 13, 19: "Be anxious for nothing, but in

everything by prayer and supplication, with thanksgiving, let your requests be made known to God; and the peace of God, which surpasses all understanding, will guard your hearts and minds through Christ Jesus. . . . I can do all things through Christ who strengthens me. . . . And my God shall supply all your need according to His riches in glory by Christ Jesus."
Colossians 3:15: "And let the peace of God rule in your hearts, to which also you were called in one body; and be thankful."

The Assurance of the Lord's Guidance

Psalm 32:8: "I will instruct you and teach you in the way you should go; / I will guide you with My eye."
Proverbs 16:3: "Commit your works to the Lord, / And your thoughts will be established."
Ecclesiastes 2:26: "For God gives wisdom and knowledge and joy to a man who is good in His sight; but to the sinner He gives the work of gathering and collecting, that he may give to him who is good before God. This also is vanity and grasping for the wind."
Isaiah 30:20: "And though the Lord gives you / The bread of adversity and the water of affliction, / Yet your teachers will not be moved into a corner anymore, / But your eyes shall see your teachers."
Isaiah 42:16: "I will bring the blind by a way they did not know; / I will lead them in paths they have not known. / I will make darkness light before them, / And crooked places straight. / These things I will do for them, / And not forsake them."

The Assurance That the Lord Answers Prayer

Psalm 145:18–19: "The Lord is near to all who call upon Him, / To all who call upon Him in truth. / He will fulfill the desire of those who fear Him; / He also will hear their cry and save them."

Jeremiah 33:3: "Call to Me, and I will answer you, and show you great and mighty things, which you do not know."

Matthew 7:7–8, 11: "Ask and it will be given to you; seek, and you will find; knock, and it will be opened to you. For everyone who asks receives, and he who seeks finds, and to him who knocks it will be opened. . . . If you then, being evil, know how to give good gifts to your children, how much more will your Father who is in heaven give good things to those who ask Him!"

John 15:7, 16:23–24: "If you abide in Me, and My words abide in you, you will ask what you desire, and it shall be done for you. . . . And in that day you will ask Me nothing. Most assuredly, I say to you, whatever you ask the Father in My name He will give you. Until now you have asked nothing in My name. Ask, and you will receive, that your joy may be full."

Philippians 4:19: "And my God shall supply all your need according to His riches in glory by Christ Jesus."

Hebrews 4:14–16: "Seeing then that we have a great High Priest who has passed through the heavens, Jesus the Son of God, let us hold fast our confession. For we do not have a High Priest who cannot sympathize with our weaknesses, but was in all points tempted as we are, yet without sin. Let us therefore come boldly to the throne of grace, that we may obtain mercy and find grace to help in time of need."

2 Timothy 1:7: "For God has not given us a spirit of fear, but of power and of love and of a sound mind."

MAKING STRESS
WORK FOR YOU

STUDY GUIDE

Read the Book of James straight through. If you can, sense the scope and core of the Book. The key verse is James 1:18: "Of His own will He brought us forth by the word of truth, that we might be a kind of firstfruits of His creatures." Everything James says in this brief epistle is designed to encourage people in the early church to turn the power of God loose in their lives. This power is available to Christians today as well. And a significant part of the power is the ability to cope. And that power utilizes the stress-coping mechanism the Lord has given us so that we can make stress work for us rather than be helpless victims of its debilitating impact.

Chapter 1: The Secret of Managing Stress

1. On page 19 Dr. Ogilvie suggests that articles and books about stress can *cause* stress. As you read through this book, how do you feel you personally can create a climate so that *Making Stress Work for You* will have positive rather than negative effects upon you?

2. As you look at your own lifestyle, do you detect any particular potential sources of stress?

3. The secret of stress management, says Dr. Ogilvie, lies in our relationship to God (page 29). What can you consciously do to enrich that relationship?

4. Why do so many Christians (as well as non-Christians) have such a high residue of stress in their lives (see discussion which begins on page 35)?

5. On page 37 Dr. Ogilvie lists "five 'C's'." Which of these five cause you the greatest problem?

6. Now that you have worked through the chapter, write your own definition of what stress is and how it works.

Chapter 2: How to Be Good and Angry

1. On page 45 Dr. Ogilvie says, ". . . so many of the popular television programs trigger our indignation index." Comment on this and try to analyse your own personal "indignation index."

2. Can you identify with the woman described on page 46?

3. Can talking about our frustrations and submerged anger help us deal creatively with the pressures upon us? How does it work for you?

4. Dr. Ogilvie quotes James 1:19–20 and lists "swift to hear, slow to speak, and slow to wrath" as three ways to handle stress-related anger. How does this system work for you?

5. Put into your own words what it means to have "the mind of Christ."

6. Now that you have worked through the chapter, list some of the things in your everyday life that have proved to be anger-producing for you.

Chapter 3: The Stress of What We Do Not Express

1. On page 67 Dr. Ogilvie talks about the problems our procrastination can create. Is there anything of this kind creating stress for you?

2. Dr. Robert Eliot says, "Don't sweat the small stuff. . . . It is all small stuff." Can you take that attitude toward your problems?

3. On page 69 Dr. Ogilvie says, "We were programmed to be a river bed for the flow of the Spirit of Christ." What does that mean to you?

4. "Freedom comes from knowing that we are loved profoundly" (page 73). Comment on the meaning of this truth to your own life.

5. Can you identify with the couple Dr. Ogilvie describes on pages 77 through 80? In what ways?

6. After reading James 1:22–2:26 and reflecting on Dr. Ogilvie's comments in chapter 3, write your own definition of "the stress we do not express."

Chapter 4: Heart Your Tongue!

1. On page 85 Dr. Ogilvie talks about "uncreative stress caused by what we say to one another." He then looks at James 3 as a striking series of

metaphors describing the uncontrolled tongue. Did any one of these speak most specifically to you?

2. How do you react to the story told on pages 90 and 91?

3. How do you "heart your tongue"?

4. Look at the fruits of the Spirit listed in Galatians 5. How do these apply to your use of the tongue?

5. React to Dr. Ogilvie's statement on page 98, "The Lord can control our tongues when we give Him our hearts."

Chapter 5: The Antidote for Combative Competition

1. Dr. Ogilvie calls *envy* "combative competition" and lists it as a primary cause of stress. Comment on this.

2. On page 103 the author says, "Competition isn't bad if it prompts us to pull out all the stops and live at our own full potential." Do you feel that you handle competition in this way?

3. The author talks about the distress of unanswered prayer on page 108, and discusses the difference between our demands and true prayer. He then calls for us to love ourselves. How does all this fit into God's plan for our lives?

4. On page 111 Dr. Ogilvie says, "Envy is really lack of self-appreciation." He then goes on to call us to "an honest recognition of our assets and liabilities," so that, "multiplied by his indwelling power, (it) will equal excellence without stress." How does that process become "the antidote for combative competition"?

5. Reflecting back on the chapter, what do you feel is the creative answer to envy?

Chapter 6: The Truth about Burnout

1. On page 118 Dr. Ogilvie points out that "it's how we do what we do, not how much we do, that causes stress." What does he mean by this statement?

2. "Burnout" can happen at every level of responsibility and does not have to be related to job stress. Why is this?

3. On page 121 Dr. Ogilvie gives four keys to living without the fear of burnout: energy, enjoyment, enthusiasm, and excitement. We can choose how we will react to life's pressures. How does the author ask us to react?

4. Our wills can be converted and surrendered to God. How does that affect how we handle life?

5. What is the fallacy of the "success syndrome" experienced by humans which the author describes on page 127?

6. How do you answer the questions the author raises on page 129?

7. Can you describe your own experience with "burnout" and your definition of what "burnout" is?

Chapter 7: Resigning from the Kingdom of Thingdom

1. Money worries, says Dr. Ogilvie, cause most of us a great deal of stress. He describes his boyhood in the Depression and his struggle to get an education, citing this background as the reason for *his* concern about money. How does your background influence your attitude toward money?

2. All of us face the financial pressure of the inflationary spiral. How do you handle that aspect of your life?

3. Dr. Ogilvie cites the stress caused by worries about retirement. How do most people handle that?

4. What about Dr. Ogilvie's translation of James 5:3 on page 146? Do you feel he's too strong in his description of the "corrosion" caused by money worries?

5. Reread the five steps for transforming our thinking that begin on page 148. Summarize them in five distinct statements.

6. Rank yourself in the following list:
   _____ I never worry about money.
   _____ I feel depressed over money.
   _____ I wrestle with the problem of overspending.
   _____ I worry about not having enough.
   _____ I fear not having enough resources for retirement.
   _____ I argue over money with my family.
   _____ Other _____.

Chapter 8: Racehorses and Turtles

1. Read the description of personality types A, B, and C on page 159. Where do you place yourself?

2. As you read about the "racehorse" and the "turtle," think about those close to you. Where do they fit in terms of their personalities?

3. Impatience is a common problem. In what ways do you reveal your impatience?

4. Dr. Ogilvie classifies the apostle Paul as a "racehorse." How would you describe the Lord Jesus Christ in terms of His personality?

5. Impatience, says the author, causes us to be judgmental. How do you handle that tendency in your life?

6. Dr. Ogilvie asks us to yield our attitudes to the Lord's control. What happens when we do that?

7. Reflecting back upon the chapter, define a "racehorse." A "turtle."

Chapter 9: How to Really Relax

1. Dr. Ogilvie calls us to meditation, to use the "relaxation response," and he shows how this process can work in our lives.

2. Why do we need to relax in this "age of leisure"?

3. Release, confession, and thanksgiving all play a part in the practice of meditation. What other steps do we need to take (see page 185)?

4. What is the last step we need to take?

5. What other steps does Dr. Ogilvie call for on page 187?

6. As you reflect upon your lifestyle, find yourself on the chart below:
   _____ I have no definite period of prayer each day.
   _____ I pray only sporadically, when I need help.
   _____ I pray only in times of crisis.
   _____ I usually pray when people upset me.
   _____ I have a consistent period of prayer each day.
   _____ I try to have a meditative period including prayer, Bible study, reflection, and journaling.

Chapter 10: Don't Take It Alone

1. Loneliness afflicts all of us to some extent. How did Dr. Ogilvie discover his area of loneliness?

2. Where are you lonely?

3. On page 199 Dr. Ogilvie calls on us to confide in " a few trusted friends." Is it hard for you to reveal your area of need to others?

4. Reread the *"Ten Things I Will Do . . ."* list and think seriously about the demands this list makes upon you.

5. Why does "the prayer of a righteous man" avail much? See page 205.

6. List the qualities you would look for in the kind of friend who could help you "make stress work for you." Are any of those qualities apparent in your life?